GO!
A Spiritual Pocket Guide for Mission Trips

Dr. Troy Dixon

DEDICATION

This book is dedicated to the countless men and women who, for 20 centuries, have sacrificed the comforts of home, the joy of family close by, their finances, and even their lives for the sake of proclaiming the gospel to the world. These are the true heroes of the Christian faith.

How beautiful upon the mountains are the feet of him who brings good news, who publishes peace, who brings good news of happiness, who publishes salvation, who says to Zion, "Your God reigns." **Isaiah 52:7**

CONTENTS

ACKNOWLEDGMENTS

This book would not be possible without the encouragement, insight, and support of three important people. My wife, Susan, who cheered me on when I woke up early to type while the house was quiet. Mike Ragland, the associate pastor who serves Normandy Park Baptist with me; his enthusiasm kept the book a priority for me. Finally, Doug Taylor, a faithful member of NPBC who proof read the original draft. His tweaking, correcting and clarifying my thoughts made the book readable.

INTRODUCTION

It is a simple command, "GO!" It is unambiguous and straightforward. It does not require much translation, explanation or application from a preacher, simply GO! Too often we take "go" and live out "come" as in, "Ya'll come and worship with us", or "come and listen to good music and hear our preacher". While we welcome any and all, our command is to GO!

As the title indicates, GO!, is a pocket guide full of daily devotions, prep guides, and evangelism resources designed to equip believers to GO! The devotions address issues related to short-term missions; they are to prepare both heart and hand for the task of serving. It is my desire that it will both encourage and challenge the missionary.

GO! Grew out of necessity. My church, Normandy Park Baptist in Jacksonville, FL, works with Word of Life: Nicaragua every year to support the local congregations' evangelism efforts. We desired to take our mission team through a daily devotion in preparation for the trip. A search of Christian bookstores, web sites, and talking to fellow pastors yielded nothing. The need became an idea. The idea was encouraged by my wife, Susan, and fellow pastors. Months of praying and writing yielded this resource.

The format is simple. The first half of the book is a collection of five weeks of devotions. Read the first three prior to the scheduled trip, the fourth is for the week on the mission field. The fifth is for the week the mission team returns home. Day six of each week is for personal reflection and journaling. Day seven is for discussion of the weeks devotions during a mission team meeting. The second half of the book is a collection of five check lists which provide further insights and advice born out of years of mission activity. In addition, there are resources for evangelism and trip planning. These resources point to *a way* of preparing for ministry, not necessarily *the way*. These have simply been helpful to prepare myself and those I lead on the mission field.

My prayer is believers will find any and every way they can to get outside the walls of the sanctuary and share the gospel. We have the eternity transforming message of love and forgiveness. The love of the Father compelled the Son to leave the glory of heaven and become a sacrifice for our sin. He commands and equips us for the ministry of reconciliation. It is time for us to GO!

WEEK ONE
OUR EXAMPLE FOR MISSIONS

DAY ONE: God Is On Mission

Max Lucado has an interesting way of depicting God's love for you. I am paraphrasing, but he says that if God carried a wallet, your picture would be in it. He might have an old picture of you from grade school, a snapshot from your trip to Disney, or even the embarrassing prom picture when your girlfriend talked you into getting a perm. God loves you so much that He would tape the finger paintings you made in Sunday school to his refrigerator door.

Allow me to carry the idea a little bit further. Imagine God's love for humanity as His passport. Several years ago, I read a tweet from a friend that offended me. He said, "You cannot claim to support missions and not have a passport."

I could not believe the audacity of the man. In my wounded self-righteousness, I thought to myself, "How dare he! There are a number of ways to support missions and not go on a mission trip. There are dozens of reasons why a person can be hindered from getting on a plane and flying to some foreign country." Though my friend would be quick to agree with both assertions, I realized he was right. His statement convicted me deeply. With all of our resources and opportunities for short-term mission trips, the average Christian in America today has no excuse for not being involved in carrying the gospel to the ends of the Earth. Reading this devotional probably means you are preparing for a trip. God bless you!

Again, let us imagine the passport of God. As you open it up and begin to investigate this small book, you notice all the brightly colored stamps in the back. They overlap and fill the pages leaving only slivers of clean space. As you begin to read the names of the countries, you realize the Lord travels a lot. Famous places like France, Australia, Japan, and Mexico show up in the book. Then you notice how many smaller, lesser known countries such as Liechtenstein and the Maldives He has visited.

He is everywhere. He loves everyone. He has already packed for the next trip; His suitcase is setting by the door. The heart's desire of the Lord is the salvation of people. This is not a New Testament, church era desire. It has always been His desire; it has always been His plan.

Read Micah 4:1-7. How many times does the Prophet use the word "peoples"? _____

It seems like a misprint or an archaic term but it is not. It is a multitude of people groups. It identifies God's will and plan. The initial covenant offer made to Abram in Genesis 12 includes the promise that "all the families of the earth shall be blessed", through him and his descendents.

List 3 ways God is shown to be consoling or benefiting people in the passage.

1. _____

2. _____

3. _____

How do the peoples of the Earth learn of the love of God?

_____

_____

My journey to the mission field actually began in a conference breakout session I had not intended to attend. I invited three men to a weekend conference on a variety of issues related to men's ministries in the local church. We had already attended sessions on leading Bible studies and weekend retreats for men. We had planned on dropping in on a training session for fatherhood. The simple instructions "go to the end of the hall, turn left, then it's the third door on your right," became a right turn and the third door on the left.

When the speaker introduced himself and began to share his love for and participation in short-term mission trips, I wondered if I was in the right place. An assistant began to distribute the materials for the session and I read the title, "Planning a Short Term Mission Trip." My heart sank. I remember thinking, "Great, I'm in the wrong place." In a few short minutes, I realized I was in the exact place God wanted me to be.

Over the next forty-five minutes, my mind was on a double track. On one track, I was listening to the speaker share the impact missions had had upon his life. He shared the number of avenues available to a church to indentify a mission need, plan a trip, enlist members to participate, and conduct the event. His handout was a road map to mission involvement.

The second track was my rebuke. It was as though I could hear the Holy Spirit saying to my heart, "You ignore missions." He was right. As a believer, I had never participated in a single mission trip. With nearly ten-years of pastoral experience at that point in my life, I had never led my congregations on a single trip nor been involved in a single project.

There were plenty of excuses to offer. We did support missions through the Cooperative Program of our denomination. With thousands of fellow Southern Baptist Churches, we funded an army of nearly ten thousand missionaries in North America and abroad. We took up annual offerings for additional missionary support. The truth was that I had not been in a mission-involved church growing up and I had continued that example. I only gave lip service to missions.

That Saturday, sitting in the wrong conference, my life changed. Conviction quickly gave way to commitment. The Holy Spirit ignited a desire that soon turned into a passion. I now pray that missions are one of the legacies of my life. My journey to the mission field began that day in a conference room in Talladega, Alabama.

What is your story? How did you get to the place where you are now, preparing for this trip?

_____

_____

_____

As you close in prayer, praise God that He loved you enough to send a witness to share the gospel with you.

DAY TWO: Jesus Is On Mission

Vice Admiral James Stockdale uttered one of the most profound lines in the history of American politics on October 13, 1992 during the vice-presidential debates. One of the most highly decorated officers in U.S. naval history, the former prisoner of war was Ross Perot's running mate in his failed bid to be president. Having had less than a week to prepare for the debate with the well known Dan Quayle and Al Gore, the moderator asked Stockdale to introduce himself. Somewhat ill prepared for the arena of politics and somewhat embarrassed by the less than presidential display of his opponents, he looked into the camera and asked two interesting questions. "Who am I? Why am I here?"

America roared with laughter. The exasperation on the face of the national hero spoke volumes. Some believed he was admitting to his lack of credentials. Most believed him embarrassed by the demeaning event. It was a gut-check moment for Stockdale.

The questions, "Who am I? Why am I here?" are simple but important. The inability to answer them is at best a formula for ineffectiveness. They could be ingredients for catastrophe, as we waste valuable time and resources on pointless pursuits. Our savior had a clear understanding of exactly who he was and why he had come to earth. Those two truths helped lay the foundation and serve as the guide for Jesus' ministry.

Confronted with the skepticism of the crowds when He pronounced the salvation of Zacchaeus, Jesus summarized His purpose and mission in a single sentence as the chief tax collector made his way back down the sycamore tree: "For the Son of Man came to seek and to save the lost." (Luke 19:10)

Jesus was on a mission. From the moment He left glory and condescended to be born as a baby into this sinful world until the day He hung on the cross offering salvation to a thief, He was always about His mission. Even after the resurrection, He sought out his half-brother, James, for salvation. His mission to seek and to save remained at the forefront of His activities.

Reflect upon Luke 19:10 for a moment. Consider the words "seek" and "save". How did those two key elements of His mission affect Jesus' life? What attitudes or activities did they necessitate in order for Jesus to be successful?

_____

_____

_____

Seeking is not a passive ministry. Seeking was not the byproduct of Jesus' daily activities. Seeking the lost meant Jesus had to be intentional in His efforts. He had to make the conscious decision to go to the places where He would most likely encounter lost people. Once He met the lost, He had to intentionally interact with them, get to know them, let them know Him. Seeking dictated that He arrange His priorities so He would be faithful to His task.

Saving the lost requires more. Ultimately, it demands sacrifice. Meeting people, loving them, encouraging them and assisting them in times of difficulty can be a help for the moment, but it does not change them for eternity. Jesus entered this world knowing that every step of His life was leading Him to Calvary. The people He met and ministered to required more than a free meal or a sickness healed; they needed their sin forgiven. That could only happen if He died in their place on the cross, taking upon Himself the wrath of God against sin. The resurrection on the third day proved the offering acceptable and our sin forgiven.

Mission is the church continuing the ministry of seeking and saving the lost. We seek them and offer them the salvation that Jesus' sacrifice and resurrection secured. The grace we have received is the grace we offer.

God wired James different. He was not like anyone I had ever met. He did not grow up attending church so he did not become a believer until after high school. He missed all the easy answers I learned from flannel board Sunday school stories and Vacation Bible School. In Bible college he asked profound questions that challenged the professors. He was always polite and displayed an intense thirst for knowledge. He simply did not like easy, pat answers. He studied the Bible with great fervor.

He also was fascinated with philosophy. Most students cringed at the thought of taking a course that they believed to be confusing and pointless. James loved to discuss the answers to life's questions that philosophers, both Christian and non-Christian, offered. He said several times when discussing philosophy, "This is where people are living".

James had a favorite activity. On Friday evenings after class was finished he drove the 25 plus miles to the bookstore in Dothan, Alabama. He would purchase a cup of coffee and head to the philosophy section. When store patrons would peruse the section, he would strike up a conversation. It would typically begin with polite questions about their interests and the books they were reading. He showed sincere interest in them. Eventually he would begin to share his views and personal faith. He was seeking the lost where he knew they lived.

What is your story? Share two ways you are actively seeking lost people for sharing the gospel.

1. _____

2. _____

Pray and ask God how you may need to make sacrifices to ensure the lost hear the good news. Record your insights below:

_____

Dr. Troy Dixon

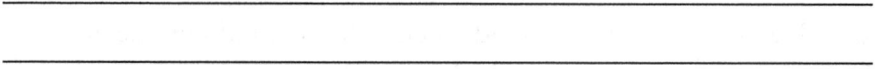

DAY THREE: The Holy Spirit Is On Mission

I have a love/hate relationship with golf. I decided that I could afford neither the time nor the money to be very good at the game. Instead, I have chosen to enjoy the few occasions when I can get out on the links and swing my clubs with some friends.

Two Waynes, both good friends, invited me to play with them. One Wayne had served my church in Alabama several years before me. The other was a deacon who served in the church. They were retired and played at least twice a week. They were both accomplished golfers. I was intimidated to play with them but looked forward to the fellowship. It was not long before they realized the declaration of my inability was not false humility. I am not a good golfer.

Around the fourth hole, Wayne Styers, the former pastor of Mt. Olive Baptist Church, asked me, almost in a whisper, if I would mind him helping with my game. I gladly accepted the offer. For the remainder of the round he would stand behind me and quietly, in a reassuring voice that was so soft only I could hear, communicate helpful instructions. He would occasionally take the grip of his club and nudge my feet into better placements or stances. More than once, he placed a hand upon one of my shoulders, hips or arms to position them better. I had more control of my game through his assistance and it shaved several strokes off my score.

Once the round was finished, Wayne the deacon was beaming at the improvement and the partnership he had witnessed. He had enjoyed watching us work together. When I thanked Wayne the retired pastor for his assistance, he deflected the praise and replied, "You did it. I simply offered some encouragement."

In fact, he was instructive but in a manner that was encouraging. Wayne played an important role in my development that day but did not want any recognition for his work. What a reflection of the Holy Spirit of God.

The Spirit is God. He is the third person of the Trinity who is fully God but takes on the role of executing the Father's and the Son's will. He works to glorify the Father and exalt the Son, yet wants no recognition for His labor. He is on mission to prepare hearts to hear, understand, and respond to the gospel. Again, He seeks no praise or recognition.

Read Genesis 24. Abraham commissioned his most senior and trusted servant for an important mission. His task was to find a bride for Isaac, the son of promise given to Abraham and Sarah. This young man was to be the inheritor of the covenant promises from God. The servant traveled to a far away land with gifts for the prospective bride. He met Rebekah and arranged the marriage.

How is this story similar to believers' involvement in missions?

_____

_____

_____

Perhaps the first similarity is obvious; the servant was seeking a bride for the son. Scripture pictures the church as the bride of Christ. (Rev. 19:7) As missionaries, we are seeking a bride for the savior.

The second similarity may not be so obvious. The servant is unnamed. Genesis 15:2 identifies Abraham's chief servant as Eliezer. This man would be Abraham's heir if there was no son. The servant assumes a mission that will bring joy to the son and does so without any thought to his own glory or self-promotion.

The mission field is not a platform for our exaltation. If the trip results in salvation for others, the glory goes to God, not us. The testimony of our trip is not what we accomplished for Him, but what He accomplished through us.

We had an observer. She was a well-dressed older woman who displayed grace and kindness in her expressions. Like a sentinel, she stood at the end of the walkway that ran from her front door. As we rounded the corner in the community of Mateare, Nicaragua, she watched us. We had just knocked on a door three houses from hers when I first noticed her. She stood, watching and smiling as our team entered the house. Thirty minutes later when we left the house, unsuccessful in leading the mother of three to salvation, our sentinel was still standing and watching us.

We stopped and began a conversation with a young 13-year-old girl. The young woman prayed to receive Jesus as Savior and Lord and we encouraged her to attend the small church a block away from her home whose members had invited us to evangelize the community with them.

As we moved down the street closer to our sentinel, I noticed her lips were moving slightly as though she were mumbling to herself. I later learned she was praying for us. She had been praying for over an hour. When a neighbor who attended the church told her a group from the states had just arrived to go door-to-door, she had begun praying.

Actually, she had been praying for over 15 years. From the time God healed her of a deadly disease and she had repented of her sin and become a follower of Christ, she had been praying. She shared her faith, told her story and prayed for the salvation of her neighbors. I thanked her for her concern for her community. I also told her that her prayers made her a partner with us. Any salvation experienced that day is a blessing to her credit.

That day approximately 10 people prayed for salvation. Probably unknown to them was a quiet, gracious woman who had been praying on their behalf for years. She did not pray for her own recognition. Her primary concern was not her own needs; rather, it was only for the needs of her neighbors.

That evening, I checked my notes for the day to update my journal and realized that we had written the names and addresses of everyone who received salvation but somehow had forgotten to write her name. So very much like the Holy Spirit, I do not think she minded.

As you pray, consider how can we be more like the Holy Spirit?

DAY FOUR: Paul Was On Mission

The spectacle produced both sadness and amusement for me. Six days before Thanksgiving I went shopping at Best Buy for a small stocking-stuffer present. As I parked and made my way to the entrance, I noticed a small village was forming on the sidewalk outside the electronics store. A sign that read "Line Forms Here" marked the village property line. On the border of the makeshift community sat a large 6 or 8 person tent that I assumed was the main residence of the village proper. Several other tents, lawn chairs, and air mattresses lined up beyond the tent in anticipation of descending upon the Thanksgiving midnight savings.

On one hand, it was amusing to observe. The residents were banding together with steely determination to fight both the ravaging Florida autumn elements and the derision of shoppers and employees who did not understand their devotion to drastic savings. On the other hand, it was saddening. They were making a significant investment of time and energy for cheap electronics. Imagine the holiday memories this will create for their children, not to mention perpetuating the idol of materialism.

If there is anything admirable in the display, it is the willingness to be in position for something perceived as important. In a similar manner, Paul sought to be in the appropriate position for the opportunities God would provide him. He understood that his life prior to salvation uniquely qualified him for his mission to the Greco-Roman people who desperately needed to hear the gospel. Since he had training as a Pharisee, he understood the Jewish Law, ceremonies and anticipation of the messiah. As a Roman citizen, he was familiar with the philosophy and attitudes of the non-Jewish population. His sense of obligation compelled him to share the gospel with everyone. (See Romans 1:14 and Colossians 1:28-29)

Acts 16:6-10 is an interesting story. On his second missionary journey, the Holy Spirit instructed Paul twice to avoid certain provinces of Asia Minor. While it was a noble desire, it was not God's will for him to carry the ministry into those provinces at that time.

Read Acts 16:8. Name the city Paul set as his new destination.

_____

Now, locate that city on the map in the back of your Bible. Notice an interesting feature about this particular dot : it was a port city.

What was Paul doing?

_____

_____

_____

    I believe he was putting himself in position for God. He did not know for sure where, but he knew God would lead. The Apostle wanted to be ready when the instructions came. From the port of Troas, the world was accessible to Paul. From there, he could journey anywhere.

    It is never appropriate to assume we know the truth about a fellow believer's heart. Nor is it appropriate to assume we know God's will for someone else's life. With that in mind let me tell you about a good friend I will call Jamie. That is not his real name; I want to preserve his privacy.

    Jamie is an incredible believer who sensed God's calling upon his life to fulltime vocational ministry. We were in Bible college together and I was in awe of him. He was smart. The nuances and subtleties of theology, philosophy, and ministry seemed to come easy to him. He was caring. He had a heart for people and sought to be a blessing to them. I heard him preach a few times and his messages were great. I believed God had His hand upon Jamie for a great work.

    The problem was that Jamie was not sure what type of ministry

God had in store for him. His first inclination was missions. His background in the medical field, along with his theological training, would have been a great help in a number of missionary endeavors. For reasons I never discovered, he decided not to pursue missions and considered serving on staff in a support position such as minister of education. He never fully embraced that idea either. He considered serving as a pastor, but the fear that he could damage the church kept him from pursuing that position as well. Eventually, my friend who was a diligent "A" student with an incredible heart for both God and people graduated and returned to his old life. He is still active in his church. He is still a wonderful husband and father, but he never followed through on his life's calling.

It is easy to pass this off as him misinterpreting the call of God, but I believe there was more to it than that. I had talked and prayed with friends who were attempting to fulfill a phantom calling. This did not seem to be Jamie. As I talked to him and attempted to counsel him, I always encountered fear. Ultimately, his fear prevented him from fulfilling his calling.

Prayer of Commitment

You are preparing for a mission trip. Fantastic! Is your commitment for a week or a lifetime? If God speaks to you on the trip and seeks you point you in a different direction, will you be submissive to his will? Write out a prayer of devotion to the Lord.

———————————————————————————————————

———————————————————————————————————

———————————————————————————————————

DAY FIVE: The Church At Antioch Was On Mission

For me it was a rite of childhood: the food drive. Every year of my elementary school education, my school would collect canned goods for less fortunate families. It was benevolence from a non-church institution. It taught me valuable lessons about helping other people. As a child, I wondered if the lesson was lost on my mother. I can remember the embarrassment I felt on the day we delivered our canned goods to the teacher. My friends would deliver string beans, English peas, and corn, both cream style and regular. From my bag, I would pull out cans of spinach and hominy grits. I felt embarrassed. I would have turned my nose up at either if it had been served to me and I was sure the recipients would be less than thrilled with their gift.

I remember the scowl on my mother's face when I produced the flyer announcing the food drive each year. The stress of being a single parent raising two children on a secretary's salary could be almost unbearable. She would mutter, "I'm not giving them our good food. Don't they know they should be having a food drive for US?" as she dug deep into the cabinets for food we could possibly do without until payday. Not understanding the weight she bore on her heart, I cringed at the thought of presenting my cans.

It may be impossible to exaggerate the importance of missions in the life of a local church. Serving others together, meeting needs and sharing the gospel builds true unity and fellowship within the congregation. It is vital to our individual maturation.

Read Acts 11:19-30. Antioch provides a great example of a church committed to missions. List the activities that you see associated with Antioch that should be associated with every church.

_____

_____

_____

I notice that they crossed ethnic barriers to present the gospel (11:20). They received discipline and direction from Barnabas and Paul (11:23-26). Later, when a famine hit Judea they raised money and sent it with their leadership team to Jerusalem (11:27-30).

We find the most humbling example in Acts 13:1-3. Antioch, which was becoming one of the leading churches of the first century, eventually attaining par with Jerusalem, risked everything for missions. When the Holy Spirit desired Barnabas and Saul to journey through the Mediterranean region proclaiming the gospel and planting churches, Antioch sent them with their blessing. When leadership is so vital to the life of a congregation, it is humbling that Antioch literally gave their very best for missions. They could have equivocated and simply received a love offering for some other mission team. They could have sent another team. Not Antioch; they gave their best for missions.

One of the challenges we face is keeping our support for missions prominent in our heart. As Southern Baptists, we are able to help with this by supporting the Lottie Moon Christmas Offering. The offering raises approximately one-half of the monies spent by our denomination for international mission work.

Mrs. Lottie was a SBC missionary to China. She turned down a marriage proposal and, at the age of 32, sailed to serve the Lord. Her ministry lasted 39 years. She died on Christmas Eve of 1912 due to the effects of illness and declining health brought on by years of sacrificing for her beloved Chinese people. It is a privilege to support an offering that honors such a godly woman.

Finding extra funds to spend at Christmas can be a challenge. My in-laws found an interesting way to keep the offering in a place of prominence in their family. They determined how much they would be spending on their two daughters for Christmas each year. They committed to give the same amount to support the missions offering. This is not the only way they support missions, but it reminds them to keep it important in their lives.

Do you struggle with keeping a focus on missions? Below, list some ways you can keep it prominent in your life. Exclude simply e-mailing a missionary on their birthday or placing a missionary's family picture on your refrigerator. How can you make missions meaningful in your life? After you make your list, pray and adopt at least one of the strategies immediately.

1. _____

2. _____

3. _____

DAY SIX: A Time for Reflection

Did you discover any spiritual/theological surprises or new insights in this week's devotions?

What new understanding of your responsibility as a believer did the devotions introduce?

What challenged your faith?

What encouraged your heart?

What area of your life are you struggling with the most as you prepare for the trip?

DAY SEVEN: A Time to Share With Your Team

Micah shows us that God has a desire for all people groups to experience salvation, do you? Did that passage reveal a people group that you have a challenge to love?

Were you convicted that you can do more to, "seek and save" the lost as Christ does? What commitment did you make to honor that conviction?

You are preparing for a mission trip; what other ways are you standing on the dock of Troas making yourself available to serve?

What did God reveal to you about yourself this week?

What did God reveal about Himself this week?

What area of your life are you struggling with the most as you prepare for the trip?

Close with prayer

WEEK TWO
PREPARING FOR THE CHALLENGE

DAY ONE: Making Your Contribution

If you pay attention to football, you become familiar with the different positions on the team. There are linemen, linebackers and defensive backs on the defensive side of the ball. On offense, you again have linemen, receivers, running backs and the quarterback. After a while, a "student" of the sport begins to realize that within the various positions there are specialists who make unique contributions to the overall success of the team.

I love the nicknames for running backs. There are thumpers, who are usually stocky, bruising running backs that excel at carrying the ball up the middle, through the defensive linemen, and over a linebacker. What a wonderful label. A scat-back is a smaller, quick and elusive runner that can dodge the bulkier, slower linemen.

The interesting thing about thumpers and scat-backs is that a team cannot build its entire offense around either style. Both are vital and play important roles, but neither can carry the entire game upon their backs. It takes the contribution of both types for long-term success.

A mission team is the same. Every trip is unique unto itself.

Even if a church is visiting the same location and working with the same missionary for several years, a variety of factors affect the trip. I believe that God forms a particular team for a particular season for a particular work in a particular location and that every member is vital to the team's success.

A challenge for the missionary is to determine the contribution that he or she is uniquely qualified to make to the team. What then follows is the consideration of how to work together in unison, people making their contribution and helping to form the team. The mission trip becomes a classroom and laboratory for the growing believer.

Read Philippians 1:1. Often, we speed through the opening verses of a Bible book to get to what we believe is the "meat" of the book. Actually, every word is inspired and should be important to us. We can learn much about God and ourselves in passages that we often treat as less important. As Paul writes to the congregation in Philippi, look for the three groups he addresses. Write them below:

1. _____

2. _____

3. _____

Now go back and note the contribution the three groups make to the life of the church.

Saints are Christians. They are not a select group of highly spiritual believers; they are people forgiven of their sins. They have an eternal relationship with God through Jesus Christ. The saints perform the work of ministry that builds the church up into "the unity of the faith and of the knowledge of the Son of God." (Eph. 4:12-13) Paul also addresses the overseers or bishops. This is the group normally referred to as pastors in the local church. They preach and teach the Bible, administer the business affairs, and see to the needs of the congregation. The third group is the deacons, who minister through service. A deacon enhances the pastor's ministry by assuming some of the responsibility for ministering to the members.

Why would Paul address the letter to these groups?

_____

_____

_____

I believe he does so to underscore the issues he will address later in the letter, in the belief that it takes all believers to protect the unity, conduct the ministry, and meet the needs of the church's membership. Congregational life, like a mission trip, is a team affair.

Typically, about mid-way through a mission trip I can identify the roles that the various members are playing on our team. Every trip I have led has an evangelist, who is not always the most obvious suspect before we leave home. The evangelist is the one who suddenly displays a heart to share the gospel with people. They cannot wait to approach another house in a neighborhood, another student at an event, or a server in a restaurant. Often fear or a perceived lack of knowledge had kept them silent in the past. Now, due to the unique location and the influence of the Holy Spirit, they share in obedience and rejoice in salvation.

Our team has always had a child-advocate, someone who cannot wait to love on the children we encounter. There is also the mom-advocate, who feels drawn to the mothers who bring their children to the kids events. The mom-advocate steps away from the group and connects with women. There are also other contributors. The team-mom makes sure everyone has water, sun screen, or bug spray. The visionary sees greater opportunities in the area for future trips. Everyone has a reason for being on the trip and can make invaluable contributions.

One of the benefits of an evangelism priority trip is the lack of specialized skills needed by the team members. That is not to denigrate the importance of the trip or the missionaries. It is the recognition that God can use anyone who is willing share the gospel. Do not forget, anyone can share the gospel.

Prayer of Commitment

In the space below, list three hobbies, activities, or interests you have that can make a connection with someone else. Dedicate them to the Lord's usage. Pray with an expectant spirit for the Lord to use you to impact both your team and your trip for the Kingdom of God.

_____

_____

_____

DAY TWO: Raising Finances

Nicaragua is the second poorest country in the western hemisphere. Managua, the capital city, has an army of poor people who have moved into town looking for help. At every major intersection, the poor offer items for sale such as origami made from folded palm fronds, fresh almonds or fruit, and cheap novelties. When the traffic stops, young children will run up to cars and attempt to convince the travelers to share a few cents or dollars. For visitors who are not used to the practice, it can be everything from amusing to saddening.

I met a young man named Kevin when I preached at the Word of Life Youth camp one year. Kevin was a support staff worker. His team had the responsibility of setting up and cleaning up the facilities. They served the meals and provided the muscle for any menial tasks that arose during the week. They made it possible for others to focus their attention more fully upon the Lord.

The privilege of serving with the support staff for three weeks cost Kevin $150. Word of Life supporters had provided scholarship funds for half the cost and Kevin was responsible for the other half. Seventy-five dollars for a poor teenager in Nicaragua is a considerable amount of money, but Kevin knew camp was God's will for his summer.

Being a teenager in a poor country, Kevin did not have many opportunities to raise his funds. Then one day he thought about the people at the intersections selling their wares. Pride would not prevent Kevin from fulfilling God's will for his life. He purchased a large bag that held several liters of purified water and smaller bags to parcel it out. He found a busy intersection near his home and began to sell water to motorists. He suffered the scornful looks of people who did not want the water. He suffered hours in the Central American heat. He suffered the ridicule of friends who did not understand his commitment. He raised his camp money.

I have heard the phrase "stroke a check" to describe paying for something outright due to an abundance of financial resources. A mission-service opportunity arises, the missionary senses God is leading, and they "stroke a check" and head to the mission field. It is a noble goal, but it may not be possible for most people. It may not be the best method for the greater Kingdom of God, either.

Raising financial support from friends and family is humbling, but that does not necessitate it being humiliating. There should not be any degradation in the process for the missionary. This may seem to be semantics, but the missionary is not asking for money. He or she is providing an opportunity for friends and family to invest in a worthy ministry.

The general goal that I have for the members of a mission trip is "three-thirds". I like to see the team raise one third of the trip expenses through team fund-raising activities such as a BBQ dinner or a car wash. The shared effort brings attention to the trip and can build fellowship and unity. Typically, sending a letter to friends and family is great way to raise the second third of the need. Again, this provides them an opportunity to participate in the work God has prepared. The final third comes from stroking a check and making a personal investment in the trip.

Certainly, the approach to raising funds is not universal. Many churches, pastors and church leaders have competing ideas on the subject. My purpose is not to enter into a debate, but to offer the thought that soliciting funds from others may benefit them. Paul received support from his family of churches and it encouraged his ministry.

Read Philippians 4:15-17. What is the general message Paul is communicating?

_____

_____

As I read the passage, I note that he refers to their support of his ministry as a *partnership* in verse 15 (ESV). Paul was the one traveling and preaching, but the Philippians' support included them in the ministry. He solidifies the thought for them in verse 17 when he says he seeks "the fruit that increases to your credit."

What are the possible fruits that an evangelism-focused mission trip can produce?

1. _____

2. _____

3. _____

To raise funds for my family of four, I sent out letters soliciting support for our first mission trip to Nicaragua. Raising funds for four people can be a challenge. It helps to have a large family, a lot of friends and three wonderful churches to have served in my ministry. The Lord helped to exceed the goals that I had established for the support letters.

Having never requested funding before, I was apprehensive about asking. All of my apprehension evaporated when the first envelopes began to arrive. Several people sent notes of encouragement in addition to their checks. They pledged their commitment to pray for our family and the mission team. There were two letters in particular that touched me.

The first letter shared a cousin's excitement for us. Several times, he had participated on mission teams with his wife and children. He wanted to give in support of us knowing the blessing we could expect from the Lord. The second letter was from an elderly member of a former church I had served. He had been active in missions for many years, but age and infirmities now prevent him from traveling. He assured me of his prayers for our team, for the trip, and for us. He sent money, as he said, "to send us on his behalf."

The support we receive from family and friends goes way beyond finances. It builds fellowship as we make our own unique contributions to the effort. I tell financial supporters, prayer partners, encouragers and well-wishers that every positive result of our trip is a blessing they participate in as well. In my dreams of heaven, I see hundreds of Nicaraguans searching out cousins, aunts and uncles, members of Normandy Park and Mt. Olive to thank them for the prayers and money they shared. With tears in their eyes, they assure strangers who are now new friends that God is pleased with their faithfulness.

Prayer of Commitment

Consider your fund-raising efforts. Has it included others? Pray for God's blessings upon each of your supporters by name. Pray that He will ignite a passion in their heart to serve as a missionary in the field where He has placed them: on the job, in their neighborhood, and with their family.

_____

_____

_____

DAY THREE: No Fear

The "No Fear" line of clothes was incredibly popular in the mid 90's. For a while, it seemed the slogan was everywhere. The extreme sports athletes wore it on their shirts, shorts and bumper stickers. That sports sub-culture included skateboarders, motocross and BMX riders, surfers and rock climbers. Their defining feature was their devotion to pushing the limits and fighting back any hint of fear in their minds.

The "No Fear" culture understands an important truth: fear can paralyze. It will prevent us from acting upon desires and convictions. Fear of what we believe can possibly happen will immobilize us from being able to accomplish what we know should happen.

Properly balanced in our lives, fear can serve as a "check engine" light or a "hazardous road ahead" sign to warn us of dangers. It may help preserve life, but it should never guide our lives.

If we have heard the voice of God accurately, then we can expect fear to whisper as well. God requires us to live by faith. That faith demands that we move past our resources, knowledge and experiences so that He can prove Himself the supreme provider, source of wisdom and dependable guide. This challenge to obey God is never greater than when we follow Him into the mission field. Fear seeks to quench the Holy Spirit's leading by causing us to focus on our limitations.

Paul wrote to encourage his son in the faith, Timothy, during a period in Timothy's life when the demands of ministry were greater than the resources of the minister. He wrote to him, *"For God gave us a spirit not of fear but of power and love and self-control".* (2 Timothy 1:7) That term "self-control" is often translated "sound mind". The general idea is that our ability to control our responses flows from our ability to understand our situation.

List 3 aspects of a mission trip that cause concern.

1. _____

2. _____

3. _____

Reflect upon this passage for a moment. To confront our fear, we are equipped with three necessary qualities: power, love, and self-control. The indispensible quality is self-control. We gain this ability when we remember the power and love of the Savior who called us to salvation and service.

Reflect upon these three provisions for a moment. How have you experienced each of them in your life in the last 30 days? Share specific events.

1. Power _____

2. Love_____

3. Self- Control_____

What an incredible provision for us. When we are ministering on behalf of Christ, the Holy Spirit empowers us. Remember that His power created the universe and raised the dead. That is certainly more than adequate for any task He entrusts to us. In addition, He comforts us with an awareness of His love. This love compelled Jesus to leave the glories of heaven. He emptied Himself of His majesty and died a sinner's death on behalf of His church. He did this because of His love for the Father and desire to bring glory to Him (John 14:31). Also, the Bible tells us He did this because of His love for His church and desire to present us to the Father (1 Peter 3:18).

The picture Paul paints for us is beautiful. Fear springs up, attempting to paralyze us with shadows of doubt and whispers of concern. In the midst of this trouble comes the reminder of God's love and power. Fear has to flee and we move forward in faith.

When God called me to preach, my life changed drastically. It required total commitment. To prepare for ministry, Susan and I quit our jobs, packed our house, grabbed our baby and moved to the panhandle of Florida. The plan was to use the equity we had built up in our home to pay for the three years of tuition at the Bible college I was planning to attend.

When we left Jacksonville, we had a contract with a buyer. The house was to close three weeks after we moved. With money in the bank, tuition would not be a problem. Instead of receiving a check, however, we received a phone call. The deal had fallen through and the house did not close. Sadly, I did not respond with faith but with shock. The shock quickly gave way to tears. The tears revealed the truth about my heart: I was afraid.

For a moment, I considered returning to Jacksonville and attempting to get my old job back. Then I did something smart: I prayed. I started asking God why. Eventually I asked what I was going to do. How were we going to make it? His answer calmed my heart. "Trust me".

In those two simple words, all my fears washed away. We had resources for the next few weeks and enough to pay the first semester's tuition. He had called me to His service and now He would care for me. Over the next three years, my Lord proved Himself the supreme provider, source of wisdom and dependable guide. Three years later, we left school with a diploma, no debt and (in my case) an extra 20 pounds of weight.

What are your fears? In the space below, honestly share the fears you have that are related to your mission trip. Let me share with you a little secret: God already knows! It might be that writing your fears down will help you realize how much greater than them your God is.

_____

_____

As you pray, remember this: there are 365 places in the Scriptures where believers are told to "Fear not"! That is a daily reminder, all year long!

DAY FOUR: Dealing with My Prejudices

Missions reveal the heart of a man. Sometimes that revelation is not pleasant. It is sad that many who claim to love the Lord and believe the Bible do not accept the call to carry the gospel to the world. A former church member spoke one of the vilest statements I have ever heard when I asked him to consider joining a mission team.

The trip was into north Mexico to help a local pastor with both a construction project and a woman's Bible study. The team would also be distributing food to the poor villagers and leading evening evangelistic services. The trip was uncommon in that it really offered opportunities for everyone to contribute in some way. One of our senior adult couples had already volunteered to go and prepare meals for the team. The couple were newlyweds, second marriages for both, at the tender age of 80 plus. They were thrilled to be going.

I asked one of our retired men who was in great health to join the team and carry the gospel to Mexico. He had some construction experience. As his pastor, I believed he would be a great asset. When I asked him if he had considered going on the trip he replied, "If I want to witness to Mexicans, I can head down to Wal-Mart."

It is an uncommon reaction for me, but I was speechless. I could not believe his audacity. It grieved my heart deeply. I wish that I could say I chastised him that day. I wish I had responded quickly with the retort, "Then why don't you?" Nevertheless, I did not. I was shocked.

Sadly, he is not alone in his prejudice; even believers carry this sin in their hearts. This is the sin of the prophet Jonah.

Read Jonah 1:1-10. Notice the use of the phrase "presence of the Lord" in both verses 3 and 10. What is that describing?

_____

_____

Psalm 139:7 asks the question, *"Where shall I go from your Spirit? Or where shall I flee from your presence?"* I believe David was saying, and Jonah was discovering, that everywhere he went he experienced conviction when he attempted to evade the will of God. Perhaps the face of every sailor on the Tarshish-bound ship convicted him. Every sailor was another soul who would find new life if Jonah would simply share with him the love of God.

Who is the person most unlike yourself that you have told about the love of God? Were they homeless or another ethnic group, perhaps a former rival or estranged family member?

1. _____

2. _____

3. _____

Penn Jillette is a magician and comedian. He is the speaking member of the Penn and Teller comedy team. He is a very articulate, well-spoken, intelligent man. He is also an atheist. I have heard him discuss current events on television several times. He has always been thoughtful in his approach. I have never heard him being dismissive or condescending when disagreeing with an opponent, and typically I agree with his opponents.

From the mouth of this committed atheist, I heard an incredibly important truth that every follower of Jesus Christ needs to embrace. Jillette tells the story of an event in Las Vegas in which he participated. At the end of the event, he was meeting fans and signing autographs when a man approached and offered him a Bible. Along with the Bible were contact information and an offer to explain the gospel and God's plan for salvation.

Jillette graciously received the Bible and thanked the man for the offer. A fan standing in line made a comment ridiculing the

Christian. Jillette rebuked the fan for his rudeness. He said that while he did not believe in the gospel or his need for salvation, he appreciated the man's concern. Then he made the comment, "Imagine how much you must hate someone to believe in heaven and not tell them how to get there."

I struggle with self-righteousness. Pride causes me to think myself better than my former church member. After all, I am willing to carry the gospel to foreign soil; I do not believe them to be less worthy of the love of God. It is in the quietness of a drive through my neighborhood that I remember the convicting words of this gracious and insightful atheist. I pass homes that are a short stroll from my front door and realize I have never knocked on their doors to share the gospel.

Prayer of Commitment

One of the most difficult requests we make of God is "show me the truth about my heart." Prejudice is often difficult to detect within ourselves. Ask God to reveal the truth about your bias and prejudices. How do you express love for others at this time? Where do you struggle? When He answers your prayer, quickly repent and allow Him to remove the barriers that sin has erected. Write out your commitment.

_____

_____

_____

DAY FIVE: The Struggle For Humility

Right up front, I have to say I am neither a "Trekkie" nor a" Trekker". Not that there is anything wrong with being a passionate fan of Star Trek; it was simply a television show I watched as a child. I saw several of the movies, but never had much interest in the spin off shows.

The original Star Trek show made one great contribution to Americana, for which I will ever be grateful; the introduction of the acting genius of Mr. William Shatner. Shatner set the standard for intense, passionate focus that found... the ... nuance... of every... line. Only Adam West or David Caruso comes close to reaching the heights of greatness established by Shatner.

I was surprised to learn that many of the cast and crew that worked with Shatner found him to be a selfish actor. According to their recollections, he sought to monopolize the attention of the viewer when he shared the screen with other actors. In an interview, a former crewmember referred to "The Shatner Spin".

Even a casual Star Trek viewer will remember the elevator doors that stood behind the captain's chair on the bridge of the Enterprise. It was in the center of the set. When Captain Kirk was coming to the bridge via the elevators, in the midst of an intense episode, Shatner would stand with his back to the bridge. As the doors to the elevator opened, Shatner would "spin" around, the attention of the viewer drawn to him and away from everyone else in the scene.

Most people crave the spotlight of attention and affirmation from others. There are a number of reasons we seek attention. The list includes low self-esteem, lack of affirmation from significant people in our lives, even the unspoken belief that we are not worthy of love. Unfortunately, church involvement, ministry, and mission activity can become a platform for people who want to impress to other people.

Read John 1:19-28. How does John answer when the Jews question his identity in verses 19-20? _____-

_____

_____

_____

Next, in verse 21, they attempt to pin him down by asking about Elijah and The Prophet. How does he respond?

_____

_____

_____

Apparently, John understood his calling as the fulfillment of Old Testament prophecies regarding "one like Elijah" who was to prepare the way for the savior. His denial of being Elijah in verse 21 was to prevent the Jews from proclaiming him a fraud or delusional.

What I find particularly interesting is John's response in verse 20 when initially questioned. Rather than provide an affirmative response, he quickly denies any claim to being the Christ. John could have explained his calling, public ministry, and success. He could have argued the benefits or theological foundation of his work, but he does not. He first humbles himself and deflects attention away. For a believer to be of any use to God, they must be humble. It has been said, "A believer will be humble or be humbled."

Where do you struggle with humility?

1. _____

2. _____

3. _____

Every man struggles with pride. Even preachers struggle with ego. There is the subtle temptation to compare our pulpit ministry to others'. The size of the congregation, the opportunities for various media outlets to carry our sermons, and the public response of a congregation at the end of a sermon all provide opportunities for ego to flourish. Preachers love to have their messages complimented.

This preacher is no different. I sought to prepare my congregation in Alabama for a series of scheduled revival meetings. Remember, we cannot schedule a revival, only the revival meetings. The last sermon I preached in preparation for it was concerning our obligation as followers of Jesus to be a vocal witness for the gospel. I shared the Biblical mandate to proclaim the good news, the example of the saints of Scripture, and the heart of God for lost people as motivation for the congregation. At the end of the sermon, we brought forward slips of paper with the names of friends and family members who needed to hear the gospel. We placed the slips on the stage steps and then prayed over them. Many of the people who received prayer actually attended at least one of the revival meetings.

The Monday night message brought by the evangelist was similar to my message the Sunday before. The text selection was different, but the example of the saints, the heart of God for the lost, and the mandate to be a vocal witness were almost verbatim what I had shared only eight days earlier. Then God reminded me of my need for humility.

After the service, I was standing with the evangelist, talking with some of Mt. Olive's members. Another member of the church drew up close to us, shook the hand of the preacher, hugged his neck, and congratulated him on a powerful, moving sermon. He smiled and assured the evangelist, "That is a message we have needed to hear for a long time."

I was both shocked and angered at the same time. I turned towards them and called the man by name, then said, "...listen to you puffing this guy up. I preached that same sermon just last Sunday morning. You sang in the choir and then sat in the balcony. I am preaching the truth; we need more people living the truth!" Then I smiled at both of them and said, "And furthermore, I have been your pastor for three years and you have never hugged my neck."

All three of us laughed and for the next several weeks, the man hugged my neck on Sunday mornings. He hugged my neck Sunday evenings. He hugged my neck on Wednesdays before and after the prayer meeting. As funny as the event was, it also humbled me. Certainly, this friend and member of my church loved Christ. He loved me and appreciated my ministry, but people do not always listen to what they are hearing. Sometimes it takes a fresh voice to communicate an old message.

Remember, we must be humble or be humbled. Humility can be a difficult character trait to possess since it requires us to deny our favorite person. Humility requires us to deny ourselves.

Prayer of Commitment

As you consider the areas where you struggle with humility, commit yourself to humbleness. Write down your action plan.

_____

_____

_____

DAY SIX: A Time for Reflection

Did you discover any spiritual/theological surprises or new insights in this week's devotions?

What new understanding of your responsibility as a believer did the devotions introduce?

What challenged your faith?

What encouraged your heart?

What area of your life are you struggling with the most as you prepare for the trip?

DAY SEVEN: A Time to Share With Your Team

What experience do you have with serving on a team? What were the challenges and benefits? Are you a good team player?

As you have been raising your financial support, how have you been surprised? Who has blessed you with encouragement or sacrifice?

Would you share one of the areas you indicated you struggle with humility? How are you overcoming the struggle?

What did God reveal to you about yourself this week?

What did God reveal about Himself this week?

What area of your life are you struggling with the most as you prepare for the trip?

Close with prayer

WEEK THREE
A MISSIONARY IS…

DAY ONE: Committed to Holiness

I had a very good friend once make reservations for me in a very bad hotel. We were in Tampa for a men's conference and needed a place to stay overnight. Rob had lived in the area for a short time so we assumed he would be the right person to find our group a nice place to stay. We were wrong.

The hotel was in an unsavory area near the interstate. The glass exit door at the end of our hallway had been shattered earlier in the evening of our arrival when the police chased a fleeing suspect in a drug arrest. Yellow police tape still hung across the hallway and doorframe.

Our room proved to be the greater problem. We had traveled all day and then sat all evening in a football stadium in the central Florida heat. We had to rise early the next day and return to the event. All we wanted was a hot shower and a good night's sleep. The shower proved to be the most difficult challenge of the trip.

As we passed the yellow tape in the hall and entered the room, we noticed how much the housekeepers had overlooked. I pulled back the shower curtain to inspect the tub and found a large rubber mat to prevent slippage. What had started out as a pristine white mat was now a repulsive dingy grey. At least three inches of mold ringed the mat in the bottom of the shower. Our group had very bad comments for our very good friend.

I folded a towel and placed it in the bottom of the tub to stand on while I showered. I did not sleep well that night since I never felt like I had really gotten clean. How does a believer live in a sin-saturated world and remain holy before God? Expressions of ungodliness bombard believers every day. This ungodliness has the ability to pollute both heart and mind. Our culture expresses itself in carnality. Pleasure and self-gratification have become the justification for any desired activity. A believer committed to the mission ordained by God has to strive to remain pure in heart, mind and body.

Read Romans 12:1-2. There is a lot of truth to unpack in these familiar and powerful verses. The first verse calls for believers to live with the attitude and actions of a living sacrifice. In short, God is demanding that we die to ourselves every day. The nature of our offering, the sacrificial life, is holy. In a few words, describe a holy life:

_____

_____

_____

What types of challenges make holiness difficult for you?

1. _____

2. _____

3. _____

Notice in verse two Paul's instruction regarding the mind of a believer: it has to be renewed. How we think, what we dwell on mentally and emotionally, transforms our lives. Paul is directing believers to be on both the defense and the offense mentally. Protect yourself defensively by scrutinizing the influences you allow in your life. Take the offense by pursuing spiritual disciplines that strengthen your relationship with Christ. Live a life that practices the holiness you possess.

Susan and I watched the last half of a television show depicting the capture of men pursuing illicit relationships with minors they met on the internet. I had heard about the show and happened to discover it on television one night after our children were in bed. It was disturbing to watch. After approximately 20 minutes, I changed the channel in disgust. I quickly decided we would never watch the show again. I watch television to be entertained and occasionally to be educated. This show did neither for us. The content of the show left me uneasy for several days. I felt dirty in my spirit.

As a believer, I must be concerned with the influences that enter my heart and mind. Discussing the influences of a man, Solomon writes, *"As [a man] thinks in his heart, so is he."*(Proverbs 23:7, NKJV) The old adage is that God will use a cracked pot, but He will not use a dirty pot. That truth is never more apparent than when we find ourselves upon the mission field.

We cannot avoid all expressions of ungodliness, but believers can limit their exposure to them. As an expression of spiritual maturity, prayerfully consider the greatest avenue of entrance that ungodly philosophies and lifestyles have into your life:

_____ Entertainment   _____ Family, Friends or Co-Workers

_____ News Media   _____ Other

How do you see their negative impact in your life?

_____

_____

_____

Prayer of Commitment:

As you consider your commitment to holiness, write out your prayer to the Lord to live out His holiness in your life.

_____

_____

_____

DAY TWO: A Joyful Worshipper

It may strain the credibility of my previous assertion that I am not a Trekkie or a Trekker, but I have attended the premiere of a Star Trek movie. It was years ago and the exact installment of the series is lost to me now, but I was there. I have a memory of standing in the lobby of the old St. John's movie theater with dozens of Trekkies. The local chapter of a Star Trek fan club was hosting a membership drive at the theater that evening and a couple dozen members were dressed as characters from the television and movie series.

A Borg stood behind the ticket collector observing the theater patrons as they arrived. Two Klingons were in line directly in front of Susan and me. They were holding a conversation in a version of the Klingon language. The devotion of the fans to these make-believe concepts overwhelmed me. Perhaps the saddest display was the two men dressed in the red tunics of Star Fleet guards. They stood on either side of the theater door as though they were guarding an important event. I remember thinking that, like so many red-shirted men on the television show; they would not survive the evening. What I was experiencing was worship in its purest form.

Worship is an expression of seeing worth, importance, or value in something. The perceived value can be seen in anyone or anything, real or imagined. There is a difference between enjoying a particular vehicle of entertainment and gleaning helpful truths from it and patterning our life to reflect that entertainment. Even if the pattern is a small segment of our life, it becomes precarious. Biblical worship is more than simply celebrating God. True worship transforms believers to become more like Christ as they encounter God.

Read Isaiah 6:1-8. This passage depicts the elements of true, biblical worship. List the elements you identify

1. _____

2. _____

3. _____

Included in the list is the awareness of the presence of God, praise for the attributes and person of God, Isaiah's awareness of his sin that leads to repentance and God's cleansing. The final element is Isaiah's response to the question, "Who shall I send, and who will go for us?" (Isaiah 6:8). He committed to go. His worship transformed his ministry.

We stood as a group looking over a sea of young faces printed on cards from Compassion International. Compassion is a ministry that raises money to support third world children with medical, educational and spiritual assistance. The ministry sponsored the concert our group was attending. The attendant at the table, a Compassion worker, found out I am a pastor and began a conversation with me. As a young couple selected a card to consider sponsoring a child, he made the comment that many of the sponsors reneged before the first year of support was completed. I thought to myself that many of our worship service commitments go unfulfilled.

God transformed Isaiah's life through worship. The burden of proclaiming faith and repentance to the Jews and the Gentiles became a hallmark of the prophet's ministry. It was the result of his response to God in worship. Many believers sense God's presence and leading in worship and make commitments. Unfortunately, the commitment often lasts just hours after the service has ended.

One of the reasons for faltering commitment is an inaccurate understanding of the nature of worship on the part of the worshipper. Too often, we understand worship as an event. We believe it is an hour on Sunday or a musical style that satisfies us aesthetically. Under these circumstances, our lives drift between periods of devotion and periods of desertion.

Worship is to be a lifestyle. We gather with fellow believers in corporate worship and live daily in personal, often private worship. Our personal experience directs us to corporate worship. Our corporate experience then fuels our personal worship. The commitments we make are not in response to guilt or new information; they are the results of understanding God's will for our lives and the focused devotion of our desire to glorify him in all we do.

Describe a commitment you felt compelled by God to make in your life that you did not honor. Why did you falter?

_____

_____

_____

Pray for a heart that remains devoted to God.

DAY THREE: Known For Compassion

Don and Ron were twin brothers a year older than I was. They lived mid-way down the street that I grew up on in Jacksonville. Both had severe vision problems. Don was legally blind and Ron was completely blind. Their vision problems never seemed to hinder them. There were many activities they could not participate in, but there were many in which they excelled. They were typical of every other boy I knew. They played ball (Ron was a fearless running back in football) and enjoyed fishing and swimming. They treated each other like typical brothers; they treated each other without respect.

One of Don's favorite tricks was to play catch with a tennis ball past Ron's unsuspecting face. When a group of boys was hanging out together, Don would produce a tennis ball from his pocket. With a few nods of his head towards his brother, he would coax another boy into tossing the ball back and forth. Each toss of the ball would pass it closer and closer to his brother's nose. Eventually Ron would hear the ball flying past and begin to yell. Once the blind boy discovered the game, his brother would attempt to make one last throw to graze his brother's face. Ron would then leap to where he believed his brother was standing. If caught, Don would be dragged to the ground for a wrestling match. All the neighborhood kids approved of the dangerous game of catch and laughed at the brothers' wrestling in the street.

We were not compassionate children. Many people still struggle to care for the plight of others. An indicator of Christ living within us is compassion for others. It should be a major factor in our decision to participate in a mission trip. Real compassion for others, a compelling desire to fulfill the great commission of Matt. 28, not the thrill of traveling to a new locale, should drive the missionary. What exactly is compassion?

Read Matthew 9:35-38. Jesus expressed compassion for the people in verse 36.

Without being tasteless in the explanation, the word compassion refers to the bowels of a person. The idea is that one's predicament and pain elicits a visceral response from someone else. The New Testament uses the word 12 times. Once it describes the Good Samaritan (Luke 10:33), once the father of the prodigal son (Luke 15:20) and once the father of a demon-possessed son who requests compassion (Mark 9:22). Every other occurrence of the word is related to God, either the Father or the Son. Unfortunately, the New Testament does not credit anyone else with compassion.

Compassion is a key character trait for a missionary. Jesus displayed an interesting pattern for believers in this passage. First, he recognized the need of the people. Second, he allowed his heart to respond to the need by displaying compassion. Third, he reacted with activity. He marshaled the disciples to pray and to minister.

I was with a group of ministry students traveling to a conference several years ago. Mid way to our destination, we stopped for gas, a trip to the restroom and a snack. The entire group walked past a man seated on the sidewalk next to the door. He was unwashed and unshaven; his clothes did not match and appeared disheveled. He was apparently homeless. The entire group walked past the man with one exception, Jerry.

Jerry slowed down when he saw the man and started a conversation while the remainder of the group entered the store. From inside the store, I saw Jerry stoop down so he could talk to the man face to face. As the team began to finish their snack selections and make their way to the cashier, Jerry entered the store and began to shop. He purchased two sandwiches and drinks. As we exited the building and returned to the van, Jerry stopped again in front of the man, stooped down and handed him the meal.

Jerry took a few more minutes with the man before he left with the group. I watched him reach out one hand and place it on the homeless man's shoulder. They both bowed their heads and Jerry was apparently praying for the man. I rejoiced to see the gesture; I hope it reminded the man that he was important to God. What moved me the most was Jerry placing his hand on the shoulder. In spite of filthy clothes and a strong unpleasant smell, Jerry showed compassion by offering the most basic form of human companionship and interaction: he touched the man.

Compassion is difficult when we begin from the position of blame. Our sinful, human nature seeks reasons to remain unfazed by the plight of others. If we can rationalize a reason why the other person deserves their circumstances, we feel comfortable in ignoring them.

The sad truth is that everyone is guilty and deserves misery. Our pain, suffering and disappointment is the fruit of the sin we choose over God. Once we acknowledge that truth, we realize we do not deserve God's grace any more than anyone else. Compassion begins at this point of common ground. It grows out of the conviction that as my friend is, I once was or certainly could be again.

DAY FOUR: An Evangelist

I heard the "good news" and did not believe it at first. My heart wanted to believe it, but past disappointments by false prophets had left me skeptical. Wanting this time to be real, this declaration of glad tidings to be true, I gave into hope.

I climbed into the back seat of a rental car with three other pastors and began our trek deep into the Ninth Ward of New Orleans seeking proof of the promise. We passed houses that still bore the damage of Hurricane Katrina over five years after the storm ravaged New Orleans. We parked in front of a run down, shabby looking building painted an uncommonly bright yellow. "The Joint" had been hand-painted on the storefront. Old rusted lawn chairs cluttered the sidewalk in front of the restaurant.

It was a neighborhood I would fear entering after dark. It was a restaurant I would consider a dive by the outward appearance. However, the power of the "good news" overcame any obstacles I could erect. My friend proclaimed The Joint to be the best barbecue he had ever eaten and I had to try it for myself.

As a barbecue enthusiast, I rejoiced when I discovered he was right. It was the best barbecue I had ever eaten. It was incredible. Since I discovered the restaurant, I have shared the good news with every other barbecue fan I know. I have proclaimed the glad tidings to friends, family and occasionally to strangers. I have returned to The Joint every time I visit New Orleans. I have brought friends and family to try it themselves.

Proclamation is the ministry of an evangelist. It is simply telling others about the good news we have discovered ourselves. A sense of obligation or fear does not motivate us, but rather a desire for others to enjoy what we enjoy. Missionaries are evangelists. They share the good news of salvation in Jesus Christ with everyone.

Read Acts 1:8. In this single verse, Jesus explains His strategy for expanding the Kingdom of God around the world. Notice that there are three important elements to the strategy. The first element is power. The church can accomplish the tasks empowered by the Holy Spirit. Let us skip the second for a moment and look at the third element, the pattern. Jesus directs the church to start local and aim global.

For today, we focus on the second element, the process. How do we convey the good news to the world? Jesus explains the process in the word "witnesses". We tell our story; we share what has happened to us. If we know enough to experience salvation, we know enough to share salvation. Study and preparation to answer questions is helpful. Memorizing verses and biblical stories enhances our usefulness. However, a lack of training should never be an excuse for silence. A maturing believer and faithful missionary is always an evangelist.

Over the years, I have learned several evangelism strategies. They are approaches to equip believers with the skills needed to explain the gospel. They are also helpful in reminding believers of the need to share. One of my favorite strategies is also the one that I believe is the most practical. The believer sticks a small red dot on their watch face over the number three.

The dot, red to represent the sacrifice of Jesus, accomplishes two tasks. The first is to remind the wearer of the need to share the gospel with someone before 3 P.M. every day. The second is to draw attention. People see the dot and ask why it is on the watch. It opens the door to sharing the gospel. The dot is a simple strategy used for years to create opportunities for evangelism.

I love the strategy. I applaud the strategy and hope believers use it successfully. I also hope I never need to use the dot. Do not hear that as a contradiction. I encourage people to use the strategy, but I hope my commitment to evangelism is strong enough that the dot would be pointless for me.

Love should be the compelling motive, not obligation. I love my wife and children. Everyone I meet discovers quickly the joy my family brings to my life. I share stories and show pictures. I probably can be overbearing with my affection for them. I share out of the overflowing love that I have.

I do not feel obligated to tell the story of my family to a new person every day. My wife does not criticize me if I do not share three family stories each day. Nevertheless, everyone I meet knows that I love my family. A mission trip is not what we do to become an evangelist. A mission trip is what we do because we are evangelists.

Whose salvation are you concerned about today?

1. _____
2. _____
3. _____

Have you prayed for them? Have you shared the gospel with them? If you do not, who will?

DAY FIVE: Known For a Servant's Heart

I did not preach the greatest sermon on the heart of a servant. I did not even hear the greatest sermon on the heart of a servant. I heard the title of the sermon and I know the preacher. The title was "Enter by the Servant's Door", and the preacher was Carl Wells. His text was John 13, which tells the story of Jesus washing the feet of the disciples. Without hearing the message, I know it was great because of what I know about Jesus and the preacher who delivered the sermon.

The title reminds us that employees and wait staff typically have a separate entrance into a restaurant. It conveys a separation between customers and staff. Business owners honor and value their customers; they seek to make their experiences special. Owners hire staff to meet the customer's needs. The title echoes Jesus' self-humiliation on behalf of humanity. The King of Kings and Lord of Lords became the servant of his subjects.

The preacher can elevate the sermon if his life reflects the message. It is also true that if he lives in a manner that is counter to the message his audience will ignore him. Carl Wells lived out humility on behalf of others for over 40 years of vocational ministry. He served several churches as minister of education and pastor. People loved him because he was Christ-like in everything he did. He humbled himself so that others could see Jesus in his life. He was a living example of a Christ-like servant.

A mission trip is about serving. When a team is working with a local missionary, they are serving to expand God's kingdom. When they are sharing the gospel with an individual, dispensing medical treatment, or working at a construction site, they are humbling themselves for the sake of others. Their activities do not provide an opportunity to highlight their perceived greatness. They are humbling themselves so others can see Christ.

Read Mark 10:45. What are the two reasons Jesus says He came into the world? _____ and _____ . You can shorten them to say He came to serve and to sacrifice. In a practical sense, the two are almost synonymous. His service found its ultimate expression in his sacrifice for others on Calvary. Since he was righteous, his sacrifice was sufficient for the benefit of others.

Can you identify examples of sacrificial service you have performed on behalf of others in the past six months?

_____

_____

_____

Donnie Taylor serves as a deacon of Normandy Park Baptist Church. He is an example of a servant leader. The word deacon, or *diakonos* in the Greek language, means servant or one who takes commands. The heart of a deacon's ministry is humility for the sake of the growth of others. As I observe Donnie's ministry, I have concluded that he has never finished a meal at the church.

Typically, he goes to refill his drink midway through a meal and does not make his way back to his seat. As his food cools off, he is walking around the room with a pitcher of tea serving everyone else. I do not believe he is consciously aware of what he is doing. He is certainly not doing it for applause or gratitude. He simply cares to serve others; he has a servant's heart.

When the meal is over, this servant-leader helps with any chore that needs to be completed. He washes tables, rearranges furniture, empties trashcans and washes dishes. He is often the deacon left with the task of turning out the lights in the building and locking doors. When members stand and idly talk as the evening grows later, he stands quietly waiting for them to finish before he completes the job.

A servant-leader rarely receives recognition for their service. They do not demand attention and most people are accustomed to overlooking someone else's humility. We live with an air of expectation. A missionary serves for the benefit of others, not recognition.

DAY SIX: A Time for Reflection

Did you discover any spiritual/theological surprises or new insights in this week's devotions?

What new understanding of your responsibility as a believer did the devotions introduce?

What challenged your faith?

What encouraged your heart?

What area of your life are you struggling with the most as you prepare for the trip?

DAY SEVEN: A Time to Share With Your Team

What is the area of greatest challenge for you maintaining personal holiness: entertainment, influence of friends, work, or schedule? How do you overcome the challenge?

Share a recent example of a meaningful private worship experience and a corporate worship experience. How did God speak to you in those experiences?

Besides your faith and family, what do you talk about with others the most? Why is it easier to talk about your hobbies and interests than your faith?

What did God reveal to you about yourself this week?

What did God reveal about Himself this week?

What area of your life are you struggling with the most as you prepare for the trip?

Close with prayer

WEEK FOUR
SERVING ON THE MISSION FIELD

DAY ONE: Eager

For some reason, I enjoy all the activities and frantic preparations surrounding April 15th each year. It is a dreaded day for most people. If you are under the age of 18, you may not recognize this as the date that federal income taxes are due to be paid to our government. Most people expecting a refund have generally had their taxes filed and perhaps even received a refund by this date. Those who owe the government will often wait until the very last minute to mail their check.

One of the activities I look forward to is the late night coverage by local media. Typically, a news station will assign the most recent addition to the television staff to do a remote report from the post office. The eager reporter will interview a post office official who will reassure viewers that if they have their returns in the mailbox by midnight, the postmark will read April 15. They will shoot video footage of the long line of cars waiting to drop their returns into the bins and interview a taxpayer who has waited until the last possible moment. It is a repetitive story that we are sure we will see again next April. No one who owes the government money is ever eager to send a check. It does not produce excitement and longing in our hearts.

"Eager" serves as a great description for most mission teams. A first mission trip or working in a new area may produce apprehension, but that always seems matched by eagerness. Months of praying and planning, raising funds and training for ministry is finally going to become ministry activity. The team members are eager to go.

A word of caution may be appropriate: be as eager to grow, as you are to go. It may sound like filler material for a thin sermon, but it can be a problem for short-term missionaries. A mission trip takes us to new places. We meet new people and experience a new culture. We become involved in activities that are not familiar to us and the adventure of the event may become more important than the actual ministry we are to conduct.

Read Luke 2:25-35. It is the story of Simeon, a believer who waited with eager anticipation for the birth of the Messiah. Notice Luke says he was "waiting for the consolation of Israel." We also translate consolation as "encouragement" and "comfort". How would the Messiah bring consolation?

_____

_____

_____

With the promise that he would not die until he saw the Messiah, Simeon visited the temple to worship when the Spirit revealed the identity of Mary's child. What does verse 30 say he saw?_____

_____

_____

Simeon lived with eager anticipation. God honored that eagerness because his focus was proper. He was not looking for a military commander or revolutionary to defeat Rome; he desired encouragement and comfort in the form of salvation. A missionary will certainly be eager to see new places and meet new people. They must keep their heart focused on the greater good, the comfort and salvation received through the gospel.

My eagerness became a hindrance to the gospel in Comalapa. We were working with Pastor Pedro, who has served the small town for a couple of years. He has faithfully ministered to the needs of his village while seeking the salvation of the city. Our team was sharing the gospel door to door, inviting people to an evening service in which I would be preaching. My desire was for our team to make contact with every home in the town. In my eagerness, I almost missed an opportunity to hear the heart of a woman who was confused about the true gospel.

Her eyes went back and forth between my wife, our translator and me as we began a conversation with her at the front of her house. It was as though she was appraising the authenticity of our hearts by looking into our eyes. She was polite but careful as she spoke to us regarding her religious background.

As we discussed the gospel, she made several statements that indicated she did not accept our assertion that salvation was through grace alone and not through good works or intentions. We would share Bible verses and illustrations, but nothing seemed to satisfy her questions. I began to grow frustrated and indicated to our translator that I was ready to move on to another house.

Suddenly she began to tell us about her life. She was Roman Catholic, but had married a Protestant who took her to the local Baptist church before Pastor Pedro began his ministry. Her husband, who later divorced her, would portray himself as godly at church and then become abusive at home. Recently she had become the target of a group of Jehovah's Witnesses. They confused her with doctrines that were counter to scripture.

As she shared her background in detail, her guardedness seemed to become pain and confusion. It was apparent she wanted to know the truth, but did not know how to be certain of it. I assured her I understood her confusion and commended her desire to know that truth. I promised her God would honor her desire to discover the truth.

We did not have the privilege of leading her to faith in Christ that day. But I believe we played an important role in helping her find clarity in a world of competing voices and ideals. She told us she believed the Bible, but found it confusing at times. We prayed with her before we left. I encouraged her to read her Bible and carry questions to Pastor Pedro. She smiled and waved at us as we made our way down her street. In my eagerness, I almost missed an opportunity to minister to her need. Be eager to go and be eager to grow.

DAILY JOURNALING

_____

_____

_____

_____

_____

_____

_____

_____

_____

_____

_____

_____

_____

_____

_____

_____

_____

_____

_____

_____

_____

_____

_____

_____

_____

_____

_____

DAY TWO: Thank God For Rainy Days

Perhaps we should blame Irving Berlin. After all, he penned the song "Blue Skies" and told us how life should be. He said, "I was blue, just as blue as I could be. Ev'ry day was a cloudy day for me. Then good luck came a-knocking at my door, skies were gray but they're not gray anymore. Blue skies smiling at me, nothing but blue skies do I see."

Perhaps it is simply our nature; we prefer blue skies and sunshine. We associate happiness with a clear spring day. We equate distress with gray skies, dreary clouds and chilly winds. It is a combination of our desire for pleasure and a limited perspective on the value of a little inconvenience.

Often our spiritual response is to *praise* when life is good, *pray* when life is bad. Of course, prayer is to be a consistent practice regardless of circumstances. The Bible teaches that praise is to be our consistent practice as well. (Rom. 12:1)

Peter provided instructions to believers who were facing opposition because of their commitment to Christ. The church he addresses, unlike that in Corinth, was suffering due to godly living, not godlessness. Peter writes these words: *"In this you rejoice, though now for a little while, if necessary, you have been grieved by various trials, so that the tested genuineness of your faith—more precious than gold that perishes though it is tested by fire—may be found to result in praise and glory and honor at the revelation of Jesus Christ."* (1 Peter 1:6-7)

List 3 trials a believer may face when he remains strong in his commitment to Christ.

1. _____

2. _____

3. _____

Notice the connection between trials and faith. Trials are

generally undesirable to us, but are useful in the hand of God. Remember, "...that for those who love God all things work together for good." (Rm. 8:28) GOD will bring a blessing out of even a dark and dreary day.

Prayerfully consider specific ways the trials you listed above can actually increase your faith in God.

1. _____

2. _____

3. _____

Santo Tomas, Nicaragua, 2012. Our mission team was working with a local church to reach a neighborhood with door-to-door evangelism. It was in June, which is the wet season in Nicaragua. We prayed as a group and divided into teams with translators. The sky darkened as rain clouds began to form. Standing on the doorstep of the first house, sharing with a man recently married, it began to sprinkle. As pastor -and not always the paragon of faith I am supposed to be- I cringed in my spirit thinking we were going to lose a day. Then God produced a blessing out of the rain.

We approached our second house as the rain increased. The man who answered the door quickly ushered us into his home. With no reason to hurry, our team began to explain the gospel. As the rain intensified into a full downpour, the father of two confessed his sin, repented and asked forgiveness from God. He accepted Christ in his humble home that day.

For the next three hours the rain continued. Occasionally it would lighten to a drizzle. Just as it seemed the clouds would pass, it would begin to pound hard again on the roofs of the homes we were visiting.

I watched up and down the streets of Santo Tomas as our teams darted from house to house, doorstep to doorstep, joyfully sharing the gospel of God's grace. Most families welcomed them in to hear the good news. My prayer is that God will give us more rainy days.

Share a time when God took a circumstance or event that seemed to be a catastrophe and produced a blessing.

_____

_____

_____

As you pray, remember this Arab proverb shared by William Barclay: "All sunshine makes a desert." Ask God what blessings, insights, and avenues of spiritual growth He is seeking to bring into your life through the intrusion of storm clouds. Recommit yourself to praising Him in all circumstances, knowing that He is greater than any storm He allows to form in your life.

DAILY JOURNALING

DAY THREE: Pity

Sometimes we have a truth communicated to us unexpectedly. Nicaragua is a poor country with its poverty apparent on nearly every highway and street corner. I began to grasp the magnitude of the problem when I saw the animals and livestock. It is normal to see cattle standing in the grass median of a major highway in the heart of town. Goats and chickens will often be standing in yards or on sidewalks in commercial areas alongside dogs and cats. All of the animals share a common trait: they are skinny. Very few of the animals appear to be malnourished, but all are slim. Even cattle raised out of town on a farm have a gaunt look to them. The most surprising for me is always the chickens. After several trips into the country, I am still struck by the sight of skinny chickens. Healthy or not, it does not seem right.

The second year we traveled to Managua to work with Word of Life: Nicaragua, I pointed out the under-fed appearance of the animals to our first-time missionaries. Ricky Verdadero spoke wisdom that changed my opinion. After pointing out the number of animals in the metropolitan area, I expressed sadness about their appearance. Ricky asked, "Pastor, how do you know our animals aren't just fat? Maybe this is how God intended them."

He was right. I know that livestock in the States is fat. A century of genetic manipulation and steroid use has produced animals that grow unnaturally fast and large for the demands of our population. All natural, free range, non-water enhanced chicken breasts are nearly half the size of their corporate co-op raised counterparts. While it is likely the Nicaraguan animals need more nourishment, it is certain that ours are over-nourished.

One of the dangers of visiting a country that is less affluent than ours is unfounded pity. Sympathy is to be expected. It recognizes suffering, injustice, and need, and produces a response from the heart. I hope that a believer will respond sympathetically to needs in ministry. Pity is different from sympathy.

Pity applies a standard to circumstances and evaluates the results. The problem lies in the standard. Missionaries proclaim the good news of the gospel, not the affluence of the American experience. The gospel frees people from sin. The gospel has the power to transform a community as hearts are changed and injustice challenged. We should never pity a people because they do not have the luxuries others enjoy. In many cases, they should pity us for the luxuries that control us.

Read 1 Corinthians 1:26-29. What are the three types of people listed who typically do not respond to salvation?

_____ .

Paul says this is God's strategy so no one can boast in His presence; no one will receive His glory. How does this change your understanding of to whom and why we should direct our pity?

_____

_____

_____

The hotel was clean. It needed a fresh coat of paint, but the owner took care of the property. The mattress was old and the sheets threadbare, but after a long day of ministry, sleep did not prove to be a problem. The next morning I discovered there was no hot water, but the cold water still cleansed me.

After breakfast and group devotion, Susan and I rode with Guillermo from the small hotel in Chontales to Santo Tomas for a day of ministry. The three of us were discussing the events of the evening and planning for the day. As we discussed the hotel, Guillermo commented that the owner was a fellow believer. When Guillermo and his wife stayed in the area, visiting churches with Word of Life Bible clubs, the owner provided rooms for free.

Susan noted the lack of hot water in the rooms. Guillermo informed her that not only did very few homes in Nicaragua have hot water; most homes did not have running water. He summarized life for the people of the country with the statement, "They have no expectation of comfort".

I am afraid that Americans have too great an expectation of comfort. Luxury and comfort too often become the standard by which we make our decisions. It is as though we cannot imagine God would ever call us to suffer want. Believers should see the dignity held by all people by virtue of their creation by God. A desire for people to embrace the gospel, not a Western standard of living, should be the motivation for missions.

DAILY JOURNALING

DAY FOUR: Dealing With Cultural Differences

Every church is different. For all their similarities, each has developed unique methods of conducting their ministry and expressing their values. Answering invitations to preach exposes me to a wide variety of congregations and experiences. Often, the peculiarities of a local church will surprise me; it is a surprise I typically enjoy experiencing.

One of my first invitations to preach was in a small church south of Chipley, Florida, when I was a Bible college student. The congregation was warm and friendly. They listened intently to the sermon and responded when I extended the invitation. As I finished my portion of the service and sat down on the front pew, an elderly deacon made announcements for the day. He called a young man forward and the church sang "Happy Birthday". Then the young man turned and slipped a dollar bill into a small box on the remembrance table. Apparently, there is an expectation of the birthday celebrant to make a special offering for missions.

As the song concluded, the congregation arose and walked to the front of the pulpit. The elder deacon turned; somewhat perplexed that my family had not yet moved, he motioned for us to come forward and join the group. Without explaining their intentions, everyone circled up and grasped hands. They began to sing "Victory in Jesus". Giving into peer pressure, my family sang along. When we got to the chorus, everyone thrust their united hands up into the air in a sign of victory. "Unique" was the word that ran through my mind.

That incident is not as interesting as one invitation to preach to a congregation with over 300 in attendance. Visitors were encouraged to remain seated during the "fellowship" portion of the service. The congregation arose and sang to all of the seated visitors a welcome song. They literally sang it to us. The people around my family turned and faced us, some even bent over to get closer to us, and several were only inches from our faces as they sang. "Very unique" was the thought that ran through my mind.

Every culture is unique. It is not a value judgment to say that the culture of the region targeted by a mission trip is different. Elements of a culture may be negative, unbiblical, or unjust, but different is simply different. Culture develops due to a variety of factors and missionaries should appreciate the diversity.

Read 1st Corinthians 9:19-23. Paul is discussing how he approaches people from different cultures. He adjusts his methods to meet their needs. He does not expect them to conform to his culture for the privilege of hearing the gospel. How would Paul approach one under the law differently from one apart from the law?

_____

_____

_____

The challenge for a missionary is being able to distinguish what is essential to the message of salvation and what is a preference of the messenger.

I became an official honorary Nicaraguan in 2013 when I drank my first baggie-soda. On trips to Nicaragua, our team often noticed people leaving convenience stores with small baggies filled with various things. The baggies were similar to the zip-lock style sandwich bags used in the States except they do not have a zip-lock top.

Nicaraguans seem to serve everything in a baggie. Children who stop into a corner store for a snack or drink can take it away ready to consume. It is amusing to see someone with a soda poured into a baggie, with the straw stood up as the top of the bag is tied in a knot. It is common to see a group of children lift a bag up and drink melting ice cream as they leave a neighborhood store. I asked our

Word of Life: Nicaragua missionary, Guillermo Aguilar, why the Nicaraguans used the baggies in such a manner. He told me that it is simply cheap and convenient.

I was making my way to the soccer field to watch the campers play the staff at the Word of Life camp in 2013. I stopped at the makeshift snack shop under the pavilion to get a drink. When I told the young woman that I wanted a cola I noticed her reaching for a small stack of paper cups. I smiled and told her no and then pointed to the small box of sandwich bags. She smiled back and pointed at them to make sure I knew what I was indicating. I nodded and she pulled out a baggie.

As I made my way to the match, several campers and staff smiled and pointed to my baggie-soda. One camper came up to me with a big smile and gave me thumbs up to show his support. As I embraced their culture, the Nicaraguans embraced me. Once the soda was finished, I found it a lot easier to slip the empty bag into my pocket, unlike a can or bottle, until I could find a trash can.

When you enter the mission field, observe the cultural differences. Appreciate their uniqueness and consider how the people's cultural expressions may meet a need or challenge they face. Enjoy the creative imagination of God expressed through the uniqueness and variety of cultures.

DAILY JOURNALING

_____

_____

_____

_____

_____

_____

_____

_____

_____

_____

_____

_____

_____

_____

_____

_____

_____

_____

_____

_____

_____

_____

_____

DAY FIVE: Breaking Camp

I do not agree with the adage, "You cannot go home again." I believe you can go home, just be careful not to overstay your welcome. For 10 years, I lived away from my parents and hometown. For 10 years, my small family would pack our suitcases, travel to Jacksonville and invade my parent's house on vacation. For 10 years, I fielded the same question from my congregation: "Pastor, how long will you be staying with your parents?"

I delivered my answer in a dry tone with a slightly grim expression, "probably a day too long". Then I would smile to assure them it was all in jest. However, it was not far from the truth. Whether the trip was for a long weekend, a quick drop in visit, or a weeklong vacation, it is hard to bring two families together under the same roof. Too many people trying to use the rest rooms, piled up around the dinner table and sitting on the furniture can wear out a welcome fast.

I love to travel. It seems that no matter where I go, I quickly begin to miss what I am familiar with at home. I miss my coffee, my recliner and my bed; I miss my home. Home is a primary blessing of God in our lives. I always love to go and I always love to return.

As the mission team packs for the return home, it does so with mixed emotions. There is sadness over the departure. Missionaries will miss the ministry events. They will miss sharing the gospel and working with the translators and local team. There is also excitement at returning to our homes and being with our family.

Solomon says in Ecclesiastes 7:8, "Better is the end of a thing than its beginning." He begins the seventh chapter of the book discussing the day of death being better than the day of birth (7:1). How can that be? How can the end be better than the beginning if you are facing completion?

As I consider Ecc. 7:8 and relate it to ministry activities, I believe Solomon is thinking about the benefit of accomplishment. A missionary returning from a short-term trip replaces ambition with evidence. They have been a part of the work God is conducting in the world. The missionary completes hours of preparation with experience.

You are in the midst of a mission trip. Reflecting upon the few days you have already served, record some of the ways the end will be better than the beginning for you when you leave.

1. _____

2. _____

3. _____

I always love to go on a trip and I always love returning home from a trip. Packing up and heading home from the mission field can be sad. You will miss new friends. You have been able to set aside many responsibilities and distractions and focus on serving the Lord. Sometimes the desire to see family and friends may lead to feelings of guilt. You may feel you are disappointing the Lord. Actually, he is the one who provided the home you love. It does not disappoint him that you find yourself caught between two places that are dear to you. I find it is easier to leave when you remember the love you have waiting at home.

After a week of ministering in Managua on my first international mission trip, four hours of total flight time on two planes and passing through three airports left me exhausted. It was after 11 P.M. when I got off the plane in Jacksonville. One more stop at the baggage carrousel, a trip to the parking lot to find my vehicle, and I was heading home. It would be wonderful to see my wife and daughter after a week out of the country with my sons.

When our team of 17 left the concourse area and entered the public access area, I heard cheers. I immediately recognized several from Normandy Park who were welcoming home teen agers and friends. I welled up in pride at the sight of our caring congregation who encouraged us with their love.

Then I saw my little curly-headed, five year old joy. My little Gracie was holding one side of a "welcome home" sign. The love of my life, Susan, was holding the other. I believed my chest would explode from the emotion that welled up in it so fast. I remember thinking, "this is why I love to come home".

Home is my primary mission field. I tell my church that we enter the mission field when we cross the sidewalk in front of the church property. Our primary mission field is our schools, our job site or office, our neighborhoods and our families. Our mission field desperately needs the gospel.

We spend weeks and months at home preparing to carry the gospel to a distant people. The Bible leaves us no choice but to go forth with the gospel. After a week away, my commitment to my primary mission field is renewed. I am always eager to go and I am always eager to return.

DAILY JOURNALING

_____

_____

_____

_____

_____

_____

_____

_____

_____

_____

_____

_____

_____

_____

_____

_____

_____

_____

_____

_____

_____

_____

DAY SIX: A Time for Reflection

Did you discover any spiritual/theological surprises or new insights in this week's devotions?

What new understanding of your responsibility as a believer did the devotions introduce?

What challenged your faith?

What encouraged your heart?

What area of your life are you struggling with the most as you prepare for the trip?

DAY SEVEN: A Time to Share With Your Team
What have you been the most eager to experience this week? What have you been the most apprehensive to experience this week?

Did you struggle with pity this week? How did you recognize the nobility and significance of this people?

Name an amusing cultural difference. Did you discover a cultural difference you want to export to home?

How is, "the end better than the beginning"?

What did God reveal to you about yourself this week?

What did God reveal about Himself this week?

What area of your life are you struggling with the most as you prepare for the trip?

Close with prayer

WEEK FIVE
OUR ONGOING MISSION

DAY ONE: Stay Disconnected

Busy schedules and changing priorities make quality time together difficult for families. The advent of social media and portable connections such as smart phones and tablets increases the challenge. Recently I was sitting in a restaurant with my family enjoying a meal together. At one point, I casually observed the other diners in the room.

There were nearly a dozen tables with seated guests. More than 20 people, in addition to my family, were talking, ordering or eating their meal. I noticed that every table had at least one person with a cell phone or tablet in hand with their attention divided. Several tables had all of the patrons distracted by their devices. I did not feel like I could admonish anyone since I had just finished taking cell phone pictures of each of my children.

One table stood out to me. A couple of senior adults were finishing their dinner with a cup of coffee. They smiled as they talked and I thought to myself that they were enjoying a quiet date night. It was encouraging to see two people who knew how to be together in the moment and appreciate each other's company.

Suddenly an extremely loud phone ring disturbed the quiet of their table. The man pulled a cell phone out of his pocket designed for senior adults. It had extra large buttons and a very loud ring tone. He answered the clam shaped phone with an equally loud, "HELLO?" He continued with the conversation for several minutes, explaining where he was and what he had just eaten. His wife turned away, embarrassed by the attention he was drawing from the tables around them.

One of the blessings of the mission field is the necessity to disconnect. Serving in a foreign country will typically make internet service either physically impossible due to a lack of signal or prohibitively expensive. Even in the States, the schedule and ministry demands of the trip will cause the missionaries to reduce their updates drastically. Disconnecting is good. It helps removes distractions.

Read Luke 5:12-16. Notice the ministry that Jesus conducted with his disciples. He had just healed a man of leprosy. That miracle produced an immediate response from the community. The number of people drawn to his message and ministry exploded. It provided him with a greater opportunity to connect with others. To maintain his balance and focus, Jesus withdrew (he disconnected for a time) to focus on prayer. He knew his ministry could hinder his fellowship with the Father.

Where are your distractions? Remember, the distractions may arise from sources that are good and beneficial.

1. _____
2. _____
3. _____

An email does not show up on my smart phone or tablet for long before I have read it and then deleted or responded to it. Once, I traveled to Managua to teach at youth camp. The Baptist camp does not have wifi and the cell phone signal is weak. I told everyone who may need me while I was gone to call Susan and she would contact me in case of an emergency.

When the trip was completed, I flew back into Miami airport en route to Jacksonville. As the plane landed, I turned on the data search on my phone. Within minutes of finding a signal, the phone began to download text messages, telephone voice mail, Facebook posts, replies, and 135 emails. I had not been able to receive anything in four days and my phone was loaded with contacts. During the layover between flights I bought a cup of coffee, found an out of the way spot to sit, and sorted through all the information.

When I was finished, 45 minutes later, I had three emails and a single voice mail that was important. There were no emergencies or major crises to address, only junk email and friendly contacts. I remember thinking to myself, "I have been gone a week and nothing major happened. Why do I need to stay so connected to everything?"

The fact is we do not. We do not need to remain so connected to so many people so often. There is nothing inherently wrong with being connected, but it can distract us from moments that deserve our greater attention.

As you return from the mission trip and are being acclimated back into your normal routine, stay disconnected. At least reduce your connections. A good rule is to reduce your posting, texting, updating and check-ins by half. Try it for a few days and see if it makes a difference in your life. You will probably find you have time to focus on your relationship with God a little more like you did on the mission field.

DAY TWO: Stay Connected

News Flash!! Men are different from women. Not to be sexist or given to stereotypes, but men are less eager to open up emotionally to other people, especially other men. They are less likely to admit they are bonding with another man or even making a new male friend. Allow me to break the mold and admit to the blessing of making new friends and bonding with other men. One of the greatest blessings I have experienced because of serving on missions in Nicaragua is the friendship I have developed with Guillermo Aguilar and Jader Arquello.

I realized how close God had drawn me to these two men one afternoon while having lunch prepared for me by Jader over a barbecue grill. I was preaching at Word of Life: Nicaragua's youth camp. Jader and I had talked about our marriages, fatherhood and our faith during the previous trips. We had even discovered a shared love for grilling out with family and friends. During the week of camp, he invited me to lunch with him and his young family. Under a small gazebo on the camp property, he grilled a large cut of beef on an Argentinean style grill for us as we talked. For two hours, we discussed books we were reading, foods we loved to grill, and the challenges of being good fathers. We bonded over types of barbecue we preferred and the blessings of Christ we enjoyed. The invitation humbled me and Jader's lunch blessed me.

It may seem like a contradiction to yesterday's devotion, but when you return from the mission field, stay connected. One of the benefits of a mission trip is the relationships you make with the people you serve alongside at the target location. Fellowship connects hearts and lives.

Read Philippians 1:3-5. Notice the word fellowship (or partnership) in verse 5. It is the Greek word, *"koinonia"*. What do you think of when you hear the word fellowship around the church?

_____

_____

_____

Perhaps you wrote about a gathering like a party or the emotional connection a congregation develops. Both of these common usages are accurate, but they are actually the byproduct of fellowship. When Paul uses the word, he is describing shared activities. In this passage, he is describing the shared ministry and proclamation of the gospel with the congregation. The celebration and emotional bond grows out of the ministry. The ministry does not grow out of the celebration or bond.

A Jacksonville sportscaster tells the story of a time when he was maligning social media in a joking tone to his son. He felt all the attention given to Facebook and Twitter was a distraction that isolated people. His son told him that in his estimation it made people closer. Distance is no longer an impediment to friendships.

Think about that in relation to the people you serve with in ministry: "distance is no longer an impediment to friendships". Through social media, acquaintances become friends and friends can develop a sense of family. You have shared ministry experiences; Christ has included you as partners in changing lives for eternity. There cannot be a greater foundation for friendship in this life than those Kingdoms -expanding activities. Stay connected. "Friend" or follow each other. Pray and chat with each other. Stay connected.

List three people you met that touched your life on this mission trip.

1. _____

2. _____

3. _____

Make the commitment to pray for them daily and, as much as possible, stay connected.

DAY THREE: The Contrast

Once upon a time, I had brown hair. Slowly the brown began to turn gray. For a while, I was brown headed with a bit of gray. That description gave way to "sort of grayish". Now I am gray. I have given up any attempts at convincing people that it is brown with gray, or even gray with some brown. It is gray. My youth has fled as my hair has changed.

What I have noticed is that as the hair has changed color, it has also changed texture. The gray seems to be lighter in weight than the brown. The brown had a bit of a wave to it; the grey at times seems almost curly. Because of the difference in the textures, I have to keep it shorter. If the gray gets long, the gray goes wild. I miss my brown hair.

There is a stark contrast between where you have been on your trip and where you are now. You have experienced two different geographies, possibly two different languages and governments, and certainly two different cultures. As you re-acclimate to normalcy, you are probably acutely aware of the contrast. The danger is in honoring one culture and mission field over the other. Certainly, there are aspects of each culture that need redeeming. There are elements that have a greater appeal to you as a person. Enjoying one local context and noting the differences is to be expected. Different is not bad. Different is not better. Different is just different.

Read Jeremiah 29:4-7. The context of the passage is different from your current situation. The prophet instructs the Jews in exile in Babylon how to operate while they are away from home. What practical instructions does he leave with them?

_____

_____

_____

For the near future, Babylon was to be their home. They were to seek to be a blessing to the Babylonians. It is very easy to see them as missionaries to this new culture.

My family owns a cabin on the Santa Fe River. It belonged to my grandfather until his death. His remaining children co-own it. I grew up spending weekends and vacations at the river. Cabin life is different. One of the first things that happens when I arrive is to remove my watch. Time and schedules do not matter when I am there. I stow away my cell phone since there is no signal. Life is slower and allows for a better focus on the river. I can spend greater time in prayer and Bible reading.

There are aspects of river life that I dearly love. Elements that I wish I could duplicate back at home. River life is not better; it is just different. It provides me an opportunity to see my normal life in a different light. Some of the things I can do when I am at the cabin, I cannot do at home. My schedule and responsibilities will not allow me. Some things I do at the cabin need repeating at home. I recognize how much a slower pace will benefit my family and me.

Life on a short-term mission trip is different. Again, that does not mean it is better, just different. How we understand people is different. We are more likely to see them through the eyes of Christ. We consider the state of their salvation first and how we can convey God's love for them. We are quicker to pray and to praise. Now that you are home, what did you live on the mission field that you are now missing? What did you practice that you need to continue? How will your life be different?

DAY FOUR: Do Not Fall Away

If you were a fan of the *television* show "24", then you know they usually handled a certain revelation the same way every time. There was a traitor working against them from the inside of the organization. Jack Bauer, the hero and main character of the show, would be attempting to stop, trace, or thwart terrorist activity on U.S. soil. As he sought to apprehend the criminals, he would realize someone was working against him who knew his strategies and plans. The camera would finally lock in on the traitor's face and the scene would go black at the end of the episode as the stopwatch ticked off the last few seconds. The intent was to make the traitor's identity a surprise.

If you follow the premise of the show, the Counter Terrorist Unit (CTU) had the task of protecting the country from terrorists. Strangely, a government agency that would ideally have the highest criteria for security clearance seemed to regularly employ at least one traitor and provide them with access to the most sensitive national secrets. They made this mistake at least once every television season. Fans of the show started each new season wondering, "Who will be the traitor this year"?

A sad truth is that often a believer will trust the Lord and follow Him to the mission field. They will sacrifice, preach, teach, and love others with great passion and then, spiritually, slip away from the body of Christ. As you return from the mission field, remember that our deployment today is no guarantee of our devotion tomorrow.

Read 2 Timothy 4:9-10. The opening words of verse 10, in the King James and New King James translation, are chilling: "Demas has forsaken me…" You can hear the pain in Paul's voice. There is certainly shock and disappointment. He does not say that Demas has left him or simply departed, the word forsaken is much stronger. At the point of real need, Demas abandoned the ministry team. It could happen to me. It could happen to you. Paul himself was concerned that he might disqualify himself from ministry (1 Cor. 9:27).

What temptations do you find in the text and from your experiences that you struggle with personally?

_____

_____

_____

The chapel was bustling with excitement. Returning students were catching up with each other after a long, hot summer break. New students were trying to figure out where to sit and how to act in such a way that they did not seem new to the student body. I had just finished my first two classes on my first day as a new student at the Baptist College of Florida and was preparing for chapel. We sang the school's hymn, listened to the introductions of new staff members and had a warm welcome extended by the administration.

The school president, Dr. Tom Kinchens, brought the first chapel message. He spoke of the challenge of faith. He commended us for following Christ's call to service. He reminded us that the challenge of accepting the call, leaving home and pursuing our education was only the first of many challenges we would face.

Then he told us to turn and look at our fellow students. As we did, he told us that half the students would be the friends we would make and keep throughout our ministries. They would be the friends who would study, serve, laugh and cry with us over the coming years. Sadly, he said, the other half probably would not. Statistically, half of the students would not follow through to graduation. Some would discover that God had not called them to vocational ministry. Some would give up when the challenge became too difficult for them. Some would make mistakes that would disqualify them from serving. Of the students who did graduate from a theological institute prepared to serve in ministry, half would not follow through to retirement for many of the same reasons. It was a sobering reality for me.

Over the next three years, I saw a handful of students leave school at the end of every semester and return home to find secular employment. They left school and many of them dropped out of ministry. Too often, when I catch up with college and seminary friends we discuss former classmates who are no longer serving. Some have even stopped attending church. It is heartbreaking and convicting. I do not want to be one of the people who give up running the race.

Do not let that be you. Do not serve, lead and leave. Protect yourself spiritually, emotionally, mentally and physically so that you are available for God to use for His kingdom. Missions should not be a destination in your journey of spiritual growth, but rather a milestone. You may never serve in this location again in your life. Circumstances in life may direct you into an unexpected area or ministry for God. Regardless of where you are in your life's journey six weeks, six months, or six years from now, make sure you are still walking close with the Savior.

DAY FIVE: Missing the Mission Field

Watching a master perform his craft is exciting. They may be an artist, athlete, musician or academic. A true master displays confidence that is the result of years of experience. I saw a subtle display of a master's confidence on a cooking show several years ago.

New Orleans chef Emeril Lagasse, at one time, had a live audience cooking show on The Food Network. On one episode he invited fellow chef Mario Batali to cook with him. The stage was set with twin stovetops and ovens. Each chef took their position behind a stovetop already outfitted with sauté pans and pots. As Emeril introduced his guest, Mario, smiling at his friend and the audience, was slowly rearranging the stovetop. Without being a distraction, he placed the pots where he wanted them for the dishes he planned to prepare. The master chef knew how he needed his workspace arranged to be successful.

The last day of the mission trip can be difficult. There is often a level of exhaustion from several days of hard work and long hours. There is the realization that soon we will be back to the routine that generally defines our lives at home. There is also the loss we will soon feel at leaving behind new friends. Leaving can be bittersweet.

More than once I have heard the pronouncement, "I could live here forever…" The missionary speaks that from the heart in all sincerity. The joy of serving the Lord without reservation and seeing the salvation of souls creates a desire to see more. What better place than the mission field they have visited? Before selling the home, ending their career, and leaving family behind, the missionary has to consider if the move is the will of God.

Read Acts: 17:22-27. Paul is addressing the philosophers of Athens. He is presenting to them a very different God and worldview than the ones with which they are familiar. Discussing Israel in verse 26, he says God determined "allotted periods and the boundaries of their dwelling places."

The immediate context is the nation of the Jews but, since God is sovereign over all peoples, the application is for us as well. What does this verse imply for where you live?

_____

_____

_____

We may not always acknowledge it, but there are no accidents or coincidences. Your home is the place prepared for you at this time. Your neighborhood is the first priority for your mission.

I sat with a young man discussing God possibly calling him to vocational ministry. It was an emotional conversation as he struggled with the decision. I asked him what type of ministry he felt called to. He told me youth work or missions. Then he made a statement he did not intended to be insulting, nor was it received that way, but it was comical. "I don't want to do what you do as a pastor; I want to do what Guillermo does as a missionary."

I realized he had a limited view of what a local missionary does throughout the year. With a smile on my face, I told him "Guillermo doesn't always do what Guillermo does." The work he is involved with the week our team is on the mission field is not the typical week for him. He only has mission teams in country six or seven weeks per year. The rest of the time he is involved in discipleship, teaching and preaching, administrative activities of the ministry and ministering to his ministry leaders. By the way, that is a good description of the local pastor's regular activities.

Perhaps you still want to stay. Consider this question: What activities are you involved with on the foreign mission field that you cannot be involved with at home? You have shared your testimony, explained the gospel, loved on people who are hurting, and made sure you had time for Jesus every day. Which of these are you not able to do at home?

Perhaps you still want to stay. Then maybe you should. If God is leading you to leave the familiar for a new level of faith and trust, then GO!

DAY SIX: A Time for Reflection

Did you discover any spiritual/theological surprises or new insights in this week's devotions?

What new understanding of your responsibility as a believer did the devotions introduce?

What challenged your faith?

What encouraged your heart?

What area of your life are you struggling with the most as you prepare for the trip?

DAY SEVEN: A Time to Share With Your Team

How have you remained disconnected since you have been home? Have you really missed it?

Who have you connected with since you returned?

What contrasts between cultures have you noted since you have been home?

How are you protecting yourself from being Demas?

Are you going to sell everything and become a missionary?

What did God reveal to you about yourself this week?

What did God reveal about Himself this week?

What area of your life are you struggling with the most as you prepare for the trip?

Close with prayer

SPECIAL RESOURCES

Preparation Guides

Planning Timeline

Mission Prayer Support Team

Sample Financial Support Letter

How To Write Your Testimony

Sharing Salvation from the Book of Romans

PREP GUIDE ONE

GETTING READY: Preparing Your Heart and Mind

This list does not include a timeline. Six months in advance of the trip is suggested for some items; others require less time. The mission team leader should provide you with a calendar appropriate to your trip.

1. **Prepare Your Testimony.** Write out your testimony and learn to share it. Be ready to share in 30 seconds or 3 minutes depending upon opportunity. (See the Resource Section on page ___ for the guide to writing a testimony)
   - Prepare a salvation testimony for evangelistic purposes.
   - Prepare a testimony of a great victory or challenge God carried you through.
2. **Learn to Share the Plan of Salvation.** Nothing is more effective than leading someone through the scriptures when explaining salvation.
   - Mark the following verses in your Bible: Romans 3:23, 6:23, 5:8, 10:9-10.
   - Refer to the Resource Guide for a suggested script explaining the verses.
3. **Enlist Prayer Support.** As soon as you determine you are going on the trip, enlist a team of 3 same gender people to pray with you. Attempt to enlist a fellow church member who is not going on the trip, an extended family member, and a friend, neighbor or coworker.
   - Each prayer partner should be a born again Christian.
   - This prayer team is in addition to the people in your immediate family, Sunday school class, or congregation family.
   - Meet with the prayer partners regularly leading up to the trip and at least once after you return.

4. **Call Your Doctor.** Make an early appointment with your physician and explain what you know of the target location and the nature of your activities. The physician will investigate the needed shots and vaccines suggested.
   - Get refills on any medicines you take regularly.
   - Pack a selection of over-the-counter pain medicine, anti-diarrhea, nausea, sun block and bug spray.
   - Ask your physician for a prescription for an antibiotic in case of emergency.

5. **Investigate The Target.** Find out all that you can about the people and location you will be visiting. Learn the history, culture, lifestyle and current events of the region. Take time to learn words and phrases in the local language that will be helpful as a visitor in the area. Get to know the receiving pastor or missionary you will be working with in the target community.

6. **Raise Funds.** It is never too soon to begin to raise funds for your trip. Consider personal projects to raise funds as well as soliciting support from family and friends.

7. **Journal.** The mission trip is a major event in your life. Do not believe that you will always remember all that happens. God works in great ways during the preparation stage of a mission trip as well as during the actual trip. He teaches you important lessons during the weeks back as he does when you are on the mission field. Record the activities, insights, spiritual challenges you face, opposition, and victories. Save it for reflection later on in your life. Journaling will bless you.

PREP GUIDE TWO

PACKING: Get it Right and Light

1. **Travel Documents.** If you are going on an international trip, make certain your passport is up to date and easily accessible. Print duplicates of travel itineraries and flight information. Often the trip leader will request a copy of your passport for their records. Make additional copies of all travel documents and stow them in a different location in your luggage in case you lose the original and need to visit the U.S. Embassy abroad.
   - Find out the rules about entry visas into the target country.
   - Find out the address and contact information for the host missionary in the target country.

2. **Be Selective With Clothing.** Have the trip leader question the receiving missionary to determine the type of clothing appropriate for each of the planned activities. Consider the climate and socio-economic level of the community as you plan your selections. Do not assume that something is appropriate away because it is appropriate at home.
   - Do not over pack. Re-wear items if possible to reduce the weight of luggage.
   - Remember that most people return with souvenirs and need luggage space to transport them.
   - Do not forget comfortable shoes!

3. **Remember Incidentals.** Pack a smaller bag within the larger bag, or a carryon bag with incidental items needed for a week. Items such as ear-buds, batteries, hand sanitizer, breath mints, daily tote bag, phone chargers,

appropriate electrical plug adaptors, and SD cards for cameras are easy to overlook at the last minute.

4. **Incredibly Obvious Item #1.** No alcohol or tobacco should be packed or consumed on the mission trip. Even if the denomination, receiving missionary and target community accept social use of alcohol or tobacco, both can detract from the testimony of the believer and trip. It is better to be conservative and leave them at home.

5. **Incredibly Obvious Item #2.** Pack your Bible. Many people now have the Bible in electronic format on a smart phone, or tablet. It is still advisable to have the Bible in material form in your hand when sharing the gospel. Select a Bible that is not too heavy for carrying all day. Select a Bible that you are familiar with and can locate passages quickly and easily.

PREP GUIDE THREE

ON THE GROUND: Remembering to be a Good Guest.

1. **No Secular Music.** This is important for the impact of the experience on the missionary as well as the target community. Make a determined effort to keep your mind guarded from any outside influences that will hinder your focus upon God.
   - Select Christian music for the trip that will encourage you to worship the Lord during the week.
   - Keep the ear buds out of your ears. Stay plugged in to the people around you; build fellowship within the mission team.
2. **No Celebrity Magazines.** The trip is to share Christ, not the American obsession with celebrity.
3. **Keep Jewelry to a Minimum.** Jewelry attracts attention and becomes a draw to crime in any culture. Poor communities can perceive it negatively and undermine the intentions of the trip. Many women will wear a plain wedding band while away and leave their expensive or sentimental items at home safely locked up.
4. **No Visible Electronics.** As you are involved in ministry activities, it is a good rule to keep all personal electronic items packed away or in a pocket. As with jewelry, they can attract crime and some communities can perceive them negatively. Attention paid to the device is attention diverted from the ministry work.
5. **Drain Your Water Bottles.** A cold bottle of water on a hot day is a blessing. Many people in poor communities cannot afford a bottle of water. When you drink a bottle, keep it close and finish the contents. Leaving a bottle half-drunk sitting around is perceived as wasteful and arrogance in many places.

6. **Keep Hand Sanitizer Covert.** Hand sanitizer is a great help in preventing sickness when exposed to new illnesses for which our bodies have not developed immunities. It is rude to meet a person, shake a hand and start squirting drops of sanitizer. Wait until you are away to prevent being offensive.

PREP GUIDE FOUR

REMEMBERING HOME: Stay Connected/Disconnected with Home

1. **Spread the Story.** Utilize social media daily if possible to report on the events. Keep the focus on God's provision for the team and moving among the target community. Introduce your world to the local mission team or church.

2. **Solicit Prayer in Advance.** As much as possible, schedule updates in advance of the trip via social media, cards, or letters with the itinerary of events so people can be praying for you.

3. **Keep Contact Limited.** Limit video chatting, texting, messaging and phone calls during the trip as much as possible. Keep outside distractions to a minimum so your focus can be on the work the Lord is doing through your team. Schedule a call home only once during the week unless an emergency arises.

4. **Avoid News and Sports.** Trust God to handle all the problems and tragedies in your hometown. Trust your team to survive a week without your attention.

5. **Avoid Drama from Home.** Encourage family and friends at home to guard what they communicate to you while you are on the mission field. Direct them to ask the question, "Does he/she have to know this immediately?" If the answer is no, then a good rule is to wait until you have returned. If the emergency rises to the level of you returning early, then they certainly should share the information. Trust God to protect and provide while you are gone.

6. **Remember Your House.** Enlist a responsible friend or family member to check on your house, collect packages and

mail, and care for pets and plants while you are away. Bring them a souvenir when you return.

PREP GUIDE FIVE

EFFECTIVE WITNESS: Meeting a New Culture

1. **Let Modesty Reign.** Dress modestly and conduct yourself conservatively. Be careful to avoid loud, outrageous, attention attracting behavior in public. The behavior may not be acceptable in other communities and could cast the team in a negative light.

2. **Help the Translator.** When you are working with a translator, speak in short, complete sentences. Generally, they have to understand the entire thought so they can rearrange the grammar appropriately for their language. Speak at a moderate pace, with appropriate emotion and with clarity.

3. **Make Eye Contact #1.** Speak to the person you are sharing with, not the translator. The translator will not be offended. If the conversation is between you and the translator, you exclude the person you are sharing with from the event.

4. **Make Eye Contact #2.** Take off sunglasses when meeting someone. Look them in the eye and smile when introduced.

5. **Check Your Humor.** Humor does not often translate between languages and cultures. The old joke, "I had a drug problem growing up; my parents drug me to church all the time," only makes sense in English. Typically, it disconnects the listener rather than includes them in the conversation.

6. **Ask More Than You Tell.** When you meet new people, especially those you are sharing the gospel with, ask questions about them and their life. Let them tell you about themselves rather than assume you already know about them and their need.

   - Cultures are different so only share your life at home as asked and then in a concise fashion so the differences in culture do not become a hurdle.

- Appreciate them as a person, not a target. The purpose is to bless them with the gospel, not add another number on a report at the end of the trip.

7. **Guard Your Giveaways.** Sharing gifts, trinkets, candy or snacks with people is a great idea when appropriate. Be careful when distributing them to be fair and equitable. Producing a bag of treats in a crowd can create a mob. Notify the local missionary of your desire and allow them to direct the activities as appropriate.

- Gifts given directly to translators or local mission team members may be inappropriate. Consult the local missionary and allow them to direct you correctly.

PLANNING TIMELINE

Up to 12 Months   IDENTIFY MISSION OPPORTUNITY

- Identify the primary trip leader.
- Consider the match of skills/giftedness between the potential team and the need of the targeted community, ministry, or church.
- Communicate the opportunity to appropriate church leaders and gain tentative approval.

Up to 9 Months BEGIN PUBLIC PROMOTION OF THE TRIP

- Set calendar dates with the receiving missionary
- Finalize approval with appropriate church leaders
- Advertise a meeting to communicate the ministry opportunity, dates, limitation of team size, and approximate trip expenses
- Set deadlines for team enrolment and trip deposit

6-9 Months   ORGANIZE LEADERSHIP TEAM

- Trip Leader
  - Oversees the work of the leadership team
  - Encourages/mentors team members in spiritual preparation for the trip
  - Serves as primary contact person for the sending church and receiving church or ministry.
- Travel Coordinator

- o Secures transportation for the team to the target location
- o Communicates the cost of the transportation with appropriate schedule dates for ticket purchase as needed
- o Investigates and communicates the appropriate medical concerns and vaccines for foreign travel as well as necessary country visas
- o Investigates and communicates appropriate travel insurance for team members
- Location Coordinator
  - o Works to coordinate the daily schedule of ministry activities and events
  - o Secures lodging, daily meals and ground transportation to ministry locations
- Communication Coordinator
  - o Communicates with the church updates on preparation progress and team needs
  - o Organizes prayer events for the church in support of the team
  - o Organizes the mission report service following the trip
- Administration Coordination
  - o Verifies passports and appropriate permission slips
  - o Oversees the collection of monies for the trip

- o Reports progress of fund raising to the Stewardship Team of the church

Note: *Several of the coordinators may be unneeded if the receiving missionary assumes the responsibilities.*

EVALUATE FUND RAISING OPPORTUNITIES

- Develop opportunities for fund raising both corporately and individually
- Present sample fund raising letters that can be mailed to friends and family
- Gain approval for fund raising activities from appropriate church leaders

4 Months

WRITE OUT TESTIMONY

- Develop a 30 second and a 3 minute testimony explaining your salvation experience
- If appropriate, develop a 3 minute testimony explaining a challenge faced, or victory experienced
- Share at least on testimony by a team member at all meetings and training sessions in preparation of the trip

BEGIN WITNESSING TRAINING

- Mark a New Testament with appropriate verses to communicate the gospel (See page 119)
- Begin to familiarize yourself with evangelism tools such as tracts, evangelism bracelets or Evangecubes, as appropriate

BEGIN COMMUNITY OUTREACH

- Practice the planned evangelism events, such as door to door evangelism, in the sending church's immediate neighborhoods
- Team members should practice sharing their testimony with friends, co-workers, and/or neighbors

ENLIST PRAYER SUPPORT TEAM

- Each team member should enlist a team of three prayer partners (see page 113)

MAIL SUPPORT LETTERS

- Submit the support letter to the trip leader for review and approval
- Mail letters with a return envelop and clear instructions

3 Months

PREPARE MINISTRY ACTIVITES

- Determine appropriate activities based upon scheduled events and age groups
- Secure materials needed and begin advanced preparation of the resources
- Prepare worship elements, such as songs and object lessons, as appropriate

2 Months

THEOLOGICAL PREPARATION

- Develop materials to prepare team members for the theological to challenges to be expected in the target communities
- Allow for time to ask questions for clarity

CONSIDER CONCERNS

- Schedule a non-agenda meeting to consider the concerns and questions the team members may have regarding the trip

MISSON PRAYER SUPPORT TEAM

Enlisting Prayer Support

1. Invite three same gender friends to unite with you in prayer for five weeks. Ideally, the three would be comprised of a fellow church member who is not going on the trip, an extended family member, and a friend, neighbor or coworker.
2. Commit to pray with each person either individually, or as a group, once per week for five weeks. Begin three weeks before the trip when you begin the daily devotional. Have them pray for you while you are on the trip. Schedule one additional prayer time once you return.
3. Share copies of the prayer guide to assist them.
4. Return the favor. Be diligent to pray in turn for them during the five weeks.

Mission Trip Prayer Guide

As the team prepares for the trip, pray that...

1. ...the team leaders will have wisdom as they plan the trip. They need the Spirit's guidance regarding travel arrangements, lodging and transportation plans, and daily ministry activities.
2. ...the leaders will communicate the purpose of the mission clearly.
3. ... each member will be able to make a contribution based upon their giftedness.
4. ...the team members will properly prepare themselves spiritually, physically and emotionally for the trip.
5. ...the team will bond as a group; support each other, and enjoying being together.
6. ...the Lord will provide all of the resources, both financial and material, for the trip.

7. ...the Lord will begin to prepare the hearts of the target communities who will hear the gospel during the trip activities.

8. ... the team will be prepared for spiritual warfare before, during and after the trip.

As the team is on the mission field, pray...

1. ... for each team member by name. Pray for the receiving missionary/ministry the team will be working with during the trip.

2. ... for safe travel from home to the mission field. Pray for safety during the week traveling between lodgings and events.

3. ... for protection from all forms of danger and illness. Pray the team will have good health and sufficient strength for each day's events.

4. ... for team unity and flexibility if plans need adjusting.

5. ... for protection and provision of the family members of the team left at home.

6. ... the team will be bold and clear as they share their faith. Pray for the divine appointments the Lord will arrange for them daily.

7. ... for the salvation of souls and the strengthening of believers. Pray new converts will be welcomed into a local church for fellowship and discipleship.

As the team returns home, pray...

1. ... they will communicate the work the Lord accomplished through the team with clarity.

2. ... they will be able to communicate the impact the trip had on them personally.

3. ... commitments made on the mission field will be honored in their lives.

4. ... they will see their neighborhood, workplace and city as their personal mission field.

SAMPLE FINANCIAL SUPPORT LETTER

This is the letter I sent in 2011 to raise support for a trip to Nicaragua. The letter covers all the basic elements important in a good fund raising letter.

Date

Friends and Family,

I hope that this letter finds you well and walking closely with the Lord. I am writing to tell you about an opportunity that is available to me this summer. I will be traveling with a 17-person team from our church, Normandy Park Baptist, to Managua, Nicaragua on a mission trip (dates___ through ___). We will be ministering to the city trying to help meet needs and present the gospel. Our team will be ministering to the patients of a local cancer hospital and area schools. We will also be leading in worship rallies during the week.

Words cannot express how excited we are to have this opportunity. I have seen the change that takes place in a believer's life when they get out of their comfort zone and realize that they are in partnership with God. He uses us to change lives for eternity. A mission trip affects our own community when the team returns home and begins to see their world with the eyes of a missionary. It helps create within us the heart of Christ. I know this week is going to be life changing for Nicaragua, Normandy Park and myself.

I am asking you to help us in two important ways. First is to pray for us. We will only go as far, and be as successful as our prayer support carries us. We desperately need your prayers. In addition, if you are able, we are asking our family and friends to help us financially. The cost of the trip is $1,200 per person for the airfare, lodging, food and expenses. That is a lot for me, so I can honestly say I need your help.

Enclosed is an envelope for your convenience. If you should decide to send a check please make it payable to Normandy Park Baptist Church without anything written in the memo line. This will make your gift tax-deductible under IRS regulations.

Thank you for giving me a few moments to share with you what God is doing in my life. I love you and pray God's very best for you!

Sincerely,

Troy

HOW TO WRITE YOUR TESTIMONY

Acts 22 records Paul sharing his testimony. He explained his life before Christ, the process of his salvation, and the change it made in him. Divide your testimony into three parts: your life before salvation, how you came to faith in Christ and the transformation in your life since.

KEY ELEMENTS

Life Before Christ: This section covers what your life was like before you accepted Christ. Consider the following questions:

- What were you like as a person?
- What was important to you?
- What challenges, disappointments did you face?

Discovering Christ: This section explains the steps that led to your salvation. Consider the following questions:

- When did you first hear the gospel?
- How did you struggle with the decision?
- What led you to accept Christ?

Life Since Salvation: This section explains the transformation of your life since receiving Christ. Consider the following questions:

- What specific changes have come about because of salvation?
- What has changed in how you are motivated now that Christ is in your life?

ITEMS TO REMEMBER

An effective testimony is:

- Concise, clear and short
- Focuses on your savior more than your sin
- Honest and encouraging
- Includes scripture; your story is the vehicle to convey the gospel through scripture.

An effective testimony avoids:

- Negative statements about other people, churches or denominations
- Undefined church or biblical terms the listener may not find familiar
- Unrealistic expectations of the Christian life such as freedom from problems or stress
- Excessive details in the story
- Glorifying past sin

SHARING SALVATION FROM THE BOOK OF ROMANS

There are a number of effective tools to use in communicating the gospel in evangelism. Gospel tracts, "evangecubes", Good New bracelets have all been proven helpful when properly used. The easiest and most successful instrument is still the Bible. Since it is the Word of God that brings about the conversion of a soul (James 1:21), a clear explanation of the scriptures is imperative.

A selection of verses in Romans has proven to be helpful in clearly communicating the gospel. Often referred to as, "The Romans Road", below is an abbreviated version of the presentation. The four verses provide a clear and concise explanation of man's need and God's provision. Underline them in advance to help locate them quickly.

Read Romans 3:23 aloud

This verse provides an opportunity to communicate two important truths that the hearer must acknowledge. The first is the reality of sin. Most people will acknowledge sin but seek to mitigate their responsibility for it. Notice Paul does not discuss the quantity, frequency or perceived awfulness of particular sins. The issue is the presence of sin. The second truth is the universal guilt of all people. It may help to explain that our sinful activities are results of a sinful nature inherit in all of humanity.

State: The Bible declares everyone is a sinner.

- **Ask:** Do you know what sin is? Any thought, deed or attitude counter to God's will or word.
- **Ask:** Does this verse include you? Yes, it says, "all have sinned".

If they cannot acknowledge the reality of sin and their guilt as a sinner then do not move forward in the presentation. To deny either truth renders oneself incapable of receiving salvation.

Read Romans 6:23 aloud

This verse explains the results of sin. It produces death. This includes both physical death- all people die- and eternal death; all people are condemned to hell. The person hearing the gospel has to acknowledge they are condemned to hell because of their sin.

There is a natural break at the word, "but" and should be explained in two phases. Again, do not proceed forward until they understand and accept the first portion. Once the "bad news" is accepted, the "good news" has meaning. The verse concludes with the promise that God offers eternal life to people.

State: The first part of this verse says God condemns sinners to death. That is eternal death in hell. Sinners deserve hell when they die.

- **Ask:** Since you are a sinner, where do you go when you die? Hell

State: This verse continues and says God offers you the gift of eternal life in Jesus.

- **Ask:** Do you want to be forgiven for your sin?

Read Romans 5:8 aloud

This verse answers a number of important questions. It explains that God can forgive us since He has already punished Jesus in our place. It explains that His love for us motivates His actions. It also points out that God acted while we were still sinners. He does not wait for us to become worthy of salvation since that would never happen. This counters the argument that a person should wait until they have improved their life.

Ask: If sin is so bad, how can God forgive it?

- **State:** Because of the love God has for you, He sacrificed his sinless Son in our place on the cross. God punished Jesus for our sin.

Ask: Are you willing to accept Jesus' offering on your behalf and be saved today?

- **State:** There is no such thing as "cleaning up" or "good enough". Salvation is available because Jesus is sinless and punished for you.

Read Romans 10:9-10 aloud

This passage explains both the need and nature of Biblical confession. It identifies a person with Jesus as their savior. Declaring Jesus as Lord means He will guide our lives away from sin. Repentance is turning away from sin and is foundational to salvation.

State: God can save you if you confess your sin, turn from it and ask Him for forgiveness.

- **Ask:** Would you like to pray for salvation?

Remind the person that there is nothing magical or mystical about the prayer. God responds to the heart, not a particular organization of words.

Dear God, I know that Jesus is your son and that he died on the cross for me. I believe he was raised from the dead on the third day. I confess I have sinned and I ask your forgiveness. I ask Jesus to come into my life as both Savior and Lord. With your help, I want to turn away from my sins. Thank You for saving me. In Jesus' name, Amen.

ABOUT THE AUTHOR

Dr. Troy Dixon is the pastor of Normandy Park Baptist Church in Jacksonville, FL. He has a passion for missions and evangelism. He is a graduate of The Baptist College of Florida (B.A.) and The New Orleans Baptist Theological Seminary (M.Div. and D.Min.).

He and his wife, Susan, enjoy leading their three children to serve as a family on mission trips.